Perceptions In Healthy Cooking

A Vegan, Macrobiotic and Whole Foods Cookbook

Revised Edition
by
Valerie Wilson

~ *Perceptions~*

All our lives
Are appointed to us
Through our own
Perceptions of the moment
Change your perception
Change your life.

Perceptions in Healthy Cooking – Revised Edition

ISBN – 9781514762455
ISBN – 1514762455

The author of this book does not dispense medical advice or prescribe the use of any technique as a form of treatment for physical, emotional, or medical condition either directly or indirectly. The intent of the author and information provided herein is only to offer information of a general nature to help you in your quest for your over-all wellbeing. In the event that you use any of this information in this book for yourself, which is your constitutional right, the author and the publisher assume no responsibility for your actions.

All recipes, poetry and photographs are the personal and intellectual property of Valerie Wilson.

Other books by Valerie Wilson include:

Healthy and Delicious Cooking Spring Season

Contact Valerie Wilson – www.macroval.com

Cover photos shot by Randy P. Cole-Koltyk.

Dedication:

This book is dedicated to my God Mother, Vivian Bottger. When the first edition of this book came out, she carried a copy in her purse with her everywhere she went and showed it to everyone. Her support meant the world to me.

Special Thanks:

I have the best Dad and Mom there could ever be, and I thank them for their love and support.

All my cooking teachers:
My Mom, Grandma, Daryl and Dave, Lenore Baum, Patty Schniers, and Christina Pirello.

All my inspirational teachers:
Dirk Benedict, George Ohsawa, Michio Kushi, William Duffy, Edward Esko and Oprah.

My dear friends for all their support: Max, Karen, Richard, Annette, Alicia and Gary Bottger.

All my students throughout the years of teaching classes.

To my sister, Laura, without whose help this book would not be, Thank you for all your time and energy.

Chef Valerie Wilson, also known as Macro Val, has been in the food industry for over 32years. She has been living a vegan, macrobiotic, whole foods life style since 1993. She started teaching cooking classes in 1997 and still teaches in South Eastern Michigan. The first edition of her *Perceptions* cookbook came out in 2001. Her second cookbook, ***Healthy and Delicious Cooking Spring Season***, came out in 2015. Chef Val hosts her own internet radio show twice a month, REAL FOOD with Chef Val, does lifestyle counseling, and is ServeSafe certified and licensed in the state of Michigan, she has been a regular writer for two holistic magazines in her state. You can watch her informative videos on her You Tube channel and like her Facebook page, Macro Val Food. To contact her and to get links to all her services, www.macroval.com.

Table of Contents

Revised Edition

In 2001, I came out with my first cookbook, *Perceptions in Healthy Cooking*, since then I have revised many of the recipes in the book. I am excited to re-release my first cookbook with updates and a few new recipes.

This cookbook has some of my most popular recipes that, throughout the years, have become my signature dishes. My **Sweet Potato Salad** has to be served at every family get together or everyone will be disappointed. Many of my students tell me they make that recipe and serve it at pot lucks and everyone is amazed that it is vegan and does not contain eggs.

The **Quinoa Salad with Walnuts and Raisins** is another recipe that is always popular when served. The **Delicata Bisque**, made with the wonderfully sweet delicata winter squash is my Mom's favorite and one we serve at our Thanksgiving family meal every year.

Some other recipes that have become everyone's favorites from this book are: **Macaroni and Mochi, Tempeh Goulash, Tofu Sausage, Kale Catalina, Squash Rings, Millet Browns, Blueberry Apple Pie, Tofu Cream Pie with Cookie Crust**, and the **Peanut Butter and Jelly Treats**.

This new revised edition includes all the recipes from the first edition, all my original poetry, all the cooking tips and nutritional information, plus a few new recipes that were not included in the original.

A Personal Note

I have always enjoyed cooking since I can remember. I believe it all started in the kitchen with my Mom when I was young. Mom showed me all the basics of how to prepare food, from baking, to boiling, to steaming. I caught on fast, and was good at improvising or substituting ingredients. It was also my job to clean up the kitchen after dinner, which I did not enjoy. It was no surprise that my first job was at a deli that made pizza, subs, and salads. Through the five years I worked and managed the deli, I was everything from cashier, to sub maker, to pizza chef. I can honestly say I loved my job at the deli, but it was at this time that I started to have health problems such as allergies, and my prolonged battle with eczema. From the deli, I went on to be an assistant manager of a restaurant, and from there I had a couple of house cleaning businesses.

Then in 1993, I read a book that changed my life. It was ***Confessions of a Kamikaze Cowboy***, by Dirk Benedict. This down-to-earth book tells the journey Mr. Benedict took to heal his body of prostate cancer through changing his diet. This truthful book introduced me to Macrobiotics and the principles of energy, I had been looking for his book for years after hearing about it, and since I don't believe in coincidences, everything happens for a reason, this book came just at the right time in my life to send me down the path of my life's journey.

I had the pleasure of re-reading Mr. Benedict's book last year. The first time I read the book, it was all about food. But this time, after changing my lifestyle and eating habits, I read it from a different perspective. I found the book very spiritual, and realized the story was all about letting go. If you have the opportunity to read this awesome book, please don't pass it up.

I then went on to work at a macrobiotic cooking school. For two years, I learned more about the food and how to prepare it properly. I started teaching cooking classes in 1997, after a brief stint as a personal chef. At first I had to change the way I cooked to be able to teach. I was used to not measuring things, a pinch of this here, and a dab of that there, substitute this for that, was how I was use to cooking. For my recipes in the classes I had to start measuring everything and writing it all down. But now, I guess, I am used to it.

I have heard many times that healthy food does not taste good, so I have gone out of my way to create dishes that taste delicious. All my students who come through my classes can confirm that fact. I also know that not everyone has time to cook, so I also try to make my recipes easy.

When you change your lifestyle and start eating food in its whole form, not only does your health improve, you also experience an awakening of your perceptions. Many people have shared their stories of becoming more in touch with nature or their spiritual side when they change their eating habits. Which is why I have included not only my original recipes in this book, but also my original spiritual poetry.

4

I have been eating and preparing healthy, whole grain foods since 1993, and am happy to report that I have never felt better in my life. My allergies are all gone now and my prolonged battle with eczema is all over with also. In addition, my whole state of being and energy calmer and more spiritual.

In closing, I would like to point out that food is one of the most important parts of our existence. It makes up the blood which flows through every organ in our bodies. It can affect our mood and how we think. The food you choose to consume is very powerful stuff. And food is the thing you do have control over in your life. You choose what you put in your mouth. So, please make educated, smart decisions when it comes to food. Make it simple and varied.

God Bless, Val

~One Gift~

If I could give you one gift
It would be to change your perceptions
And live your life without fear.

Introduction

I would like to explain a little about energy in our food. Everything is made up of energy. In fact, everything is made up of two opposite energies existing in the same space at the same time. These energies exist in everything in varying degrees. One of the two is more prominent, so we can classify things according to the energy that is most dominant. We call these two energies yin and yang. Yin energy is expansive and moves in an upwards direction. Yang energy is constrictive and moves in a downward direction. Yin is cold, yang is hot. Yin is wet, yang is dry. Yin is sweet, yang is salty.

In food, we classify foods according to their energies. Picture in your mind a teeter totter. On the left side, imagine the yin energy, on the right, imagine the yang energy. Foods that have strong yin or yang energies will be at the very end of the teeter totter. In the middle will be more balanced energy foods, where the energies are more equal. On the left (yin) side, would be foods such as, white refined sugar, artificial sweeteners, white flour, and foods that contain those ingredients. On the right (yang) side would be, your meats (beef, pork, chicken), eggs, and salty snacks (potato chips, crackers). Now if you eat these extreme energy foods, your teeter totter will swing back and forth, up and down, going from one extreme to another. This creates chaotic energy. Let's now look at the middle of the teeter totter. This is where you will find plant based foods.

The yin and yang energy in these foods are more balanced, or more equal. This is where you will find whole grains, beans, vegetables, and sea vegetables. If you choose to eat foods from the middle of the teeter totter, wouldn't it make more sense that your energy would be calmer? As opposed to the extreme energy foods at the ends of the teeter totter that would create going from one extreme to the other, thus creating chaotic energy.

I find this study of energy extremely interesting. I have briefly explained the basics to you, but there is so much more to learn about this study of energy. There are many books on this subject; *The Macrobiotic Way*, by Michio Kushi, *You Are All Sanpaku,* by George Ohsawa and William Duffy, *Confessions of a Kamikaze Cowboy*, by Dirk Benedict. Please get them and read more about this interesting subject.

To Be or Not To Be.....A Vegetarian

Unless you live in a cave, I'm sure you have heard that eating too much meat is not a healthy thing. Doctors and scientists are now saying that high-fat food, such as meat, clogs the arteries and can lead to heart disease. This is only one convincing argument for becoming a vegetarian. If you have ever seen pictures of the appalling conditions that animals are raised in for our consumption, I know you would be turned off of eating meat.

The animals are not only kept in small cages, unable to move around, but also fed unnatural foods. The foods they are fed, along with the growth hormones, are intended to make them grow faster and get bigger.

This totally unnatural life these animals lead has given way to crazy animals, unnatural bacteria in meat, and cancer found in about 90% of all chicken sold for human consumption.

So, should you be a vegetarian? Only you can decide. It is more than a healthy decision, it is a soul decision. What you think, effects your health more than anything else. So, when asking this very important question, make sure your thoughts and actions agree with each other. I know people who decide to go vegetarian, but then feel like there is something missing. They worry that they are depriving their bodies of this or that because that is the world's perception. Eventually they end up producing a deficiency in their bodies because that is what they believe. So, when asking yourself this question, do some research and find out what is your truth. Being a vegetarian is a personal decision that you have to make at a soul level.

Organic

When purchasing, organic food means that the food is produced without chemicals. The food has been grown without pesticides sprayed on them and without chemical fertilizers. It also means no genetically modified organisms are allowed in the food. Why is this important to you?

First of all, the chemicals they use are not tested for their long term effects. Only after people have been eating food with chemicals for a long time do they see any side effects, and by then, it is probably too late. Most of the chemicals have been shown to be carcinogens.

These chemicals are not natural. They are used to kill bugs. So, logically, if they kill bugs, and we digest them, then how long will it be before they will have some ill effect on our body? Second, these chemicals have a bad effect on the environment. By spraying to get rid of one bug, another bigger, better bug comes along. The bigger and better bug will do worse damage to the crops than the first ones we were trying to get rid of. Once again, let's not mess with nature. There is a fragile balance of things in nature and if we mess with it, something unnatural and detrimental will happen. A couple hundred years ago, no one used chemicals to spray their crops and they seemed to have done just fine. They were able to grow food and have enough to eat without the bugs eating up their crops. That is because they used a natural way to control the bugs.

There are many reasons to buy organic food, but the best one I can think of is the taste. When you buy organic vegetables, the taste is so sweet and flavorful. Try a comparison of an organic carrot and non-organic carrot. The organic one is going to be sweet and wonderful. The non-organic one will be bitter to the taste. And when it comes to fruit, you cannot even compare the two. The organic ones are sweet and juicy.

I had a student who, after attending one of my classes, went home and made one of the recipes in the class. It was a dessert using raspberries. The next time I saw her, she told me that her dessert had come out terrible. Instead of being sweet, it tasted bitter. After talking with her, I learned she had used raspberries bought at the local grocery store, not organic. The raspberries had turned her whole dessert bitter, instead of the sweet dessert I had made with organic raspberries. So, next time you are at the store, remember that you deserve only the best. Buy those organic items for your health, well-being and for your taste buds.

Flour

When using flour in your recipes you want to look for whole grain flours. Try to avoid bleached or enriched flour. When writing this book the first time, I used whole grain barley flour. It is light in texture and make a wonderful cake or pie crust. I also used spelt flour in many of my dessert recipes. Spelt is an ancient variety of wheat that has not been hybrid the way wheat has, because of this many people who have an allergy to wheat, have no reaction to spelt. If you do not have any allergies, whole wheat pastry flour makes great cake, muffins, and cookies.

If you are looking for a gluten-free whole grain flour, oat flour works very well. I have used oat flour in all the recipes in this cookbook and the taste and texture is great. You can substitute oat flour for any recipe in this cookbook.

Sweeteners

I don't recommend or use processed, refined white sugar in my cooking. White sugar spikes your blood sugar level and can contribute to many diseases. Instead I use grain sweeteners. Brown rice syrup is the most versatile and easiest to use. It comes from whole brown rice. Through a process of cooking the rice down, it becomes a thick syrup. Unlike processed sugar, it does not spike your blood sugar level. Also brown rice syrup is easier to digest and hypo-allergenic.

Another grain sweetener is barley malt. Made from the whole grain barley, it has a little bitter taste to it and I use it when I want a molasses taste. Amazake, another whole grain sweetener, is made of fermented, sweet brown rice. It has a consistency like a malt. Occasionally I use maple syrup when I want to add a little more sweetness to a recipe. The sugar in the whole grain sweeteners is maltose. The sugar in maple syrup is sucrose. Maltose will never spike your blood sugar, making it the healthiest sweetener you can use in your healthy lifestyle.

Oils and Fats

Good quality vegetable oils are important in a grain based vegetarian diet. Fats and oils have gotten a bad rap in the last few years, but you need some good quality fat in your diet. Fats can be a source of warmth during the cold winter months.

Naturally extracted, unrefined vegetable oils can help strengthen cell and capillary structure, plus lubricate the skin and hair. They can contribute taste, fatty acids, vitamins A and E, and lecithin, which helps break down cholesterol deposits in the tissues of the body. The good quality fats are unsaturated, like your vegetable oils. The bad quality fats would be your saturated fats, which would be your animal fats, butter, cheese, milk etc. When choosing your oils look for unrefined as opposed to refined. Refining the oils gives them a longer shelf life, but also removes the color, taste, and natural odor if the oil. They also remove the fatty acids, bleach it, and deodorize the oil. Also check to see what extraction method was used to produce the oil. You want the label to say 'expeller pressed' or 'pure pressed'. This means they did not use excessive heat to produce the oil, which creates hydrogenated oils. Hydrogenated oils contain trans-fatty acids which may raise cholesterol.

For sautés, I love toasted sesame oil. It has a fabulous taste that you can't beat. It also contains linoleic acid, which is the most important of the three essential fatty acids our body cannot produce.

Dairy Products

I do not use dairy products in my cooking for many different reasons. Dairy products contain saturated fat which not only causes weight gain, but also elevates cholesterol levels. This can lead to fatty deposits in the arteries, which raises the risk of heart attack and strokes.

Another reason to stay away from dairy products is the allergic reaction most people experience from them. There are more than 25 proteins in milk that can lead to various problems, such as eczema, asthma, ear infections, bronchitis and sinusitis. There is also the issue of the growth hormones and antibiotics that they force the cows to eat that end up in all dairy products. I find it very interesting to note that 300 years ago they were fortunate to receive just one quart of milk a day from a cow. Today, thanks to growth hormones and selective breeding, they can get up to 50 quarts of milk a day from a cow. I think that says a lot about how unnatural dairy products are today.

Lastly, I would like to point out that milk comes from a cow and is intended for a baby calf. I don't know about you, but I am not a baby calf. We are the only species on the planet who still consumes milk after we are weaned off our mother's milk. And it is not even human milk. (What would people think if they squeezed 50 quarts of milk out of a human mother to feed the cow population?) It appears we are breaking a major natural law. And we know what happens if we go against nature, we always end up paying for it one way or another.

I prefer rice drinks for their taste and smooth texture. There is a specific definition of 'milk', which is why in my cookbook I use the term, 'rice drink' as a milk substitute.

Night Shades

As a general rule, I do not use night shade vegetables in my cooking. I do occasionally, use them for special dishes. Many people have seen dramatic results in the reduction of pain due to arthritis and fibromyalgia, after cutting back, or not consuming them in their diets. Night shades contain oxalic acid, which binds with calcium in our body, which leads to calcification or arthritis. An occasional one of these night shades probably will not hurt you, but our modern diets have been geared to include these foods as a major part. Here is a list of the night shades: tomatoes, white potatoes, eggplant, all peppers, beet greens, spinach, Swiss chard, avocados, coconut, and tobacco.

These night shades also contain toxins. Potatoes contain solonates, and tomatoes contain tomatotine, which are both toxins. And it is interesting to note that tomatoes, when first introduced to the Europeans in 1500 -1600's, they got a very cold reception. At first they thought tomatoes were poisonous. And white potatoes were considered very low grade food and fed to live stock.

Bibliography: *"The Case Against Dairy"* in *"Vegetarian Times"*, October 1998; ***Milk, The Deadly Poison***, Robert Cohen; ***The New Whole Foods Encyclopedia***, Rebecca Wood; ***The Macrobiotic Way***, Michio Kushi; ***Shopper's Guide to Natural Foods***, from the editors of *East West Journal*.

Whole Grains

Whole Grains

Whole grains are exactly what the words say, 'whole grains'. They literally mean to eat the grain in its natural form, whole, not what has been refined or processed. The whole grain contains the bran and germ, which is where all the vitamins and minerals are located. Whole grains are your complex carbohydrates. Complex carbohydrates give us a steady stream of energy by releasing glucose into our blood stream at a slow rate. Simple carbohydrates spike our blood sugar levels and create imbalances. Whole grains are what our diets should be based around. All of our ancestor's diets were based in whole grains. When we started refining them and cutting them out of our diets is when we started to have deficiencies in our bodies. The majority of your total dietary intake should consist of whole grains, 50-60%. Your body needs a steady supply of complex carbohydrates because it can only store a small reserve of them.

Cooking Whole Grains

All grains can be pot boiled, each one having different times for the boiling. You can also pressure cook your grains which has its advantages, but I feel pot boiling is easier. To pot boil the grains, first bring the water and grains to a boil in a pot with the lid off, for a couple minutes. Add a pinch of sea salt. Reduce the heat to the lowest possible temperature. Put lid on, and simmer for the appropriate amount of time for the grain. The grain is done when all the water has been absorbed.

~Celebrate the Day~

Celebrate the day, so full of life
Celebrate the day, with abundance on the horizon
Celebrate the day, where you can see God's master plan
Of the Earth and the Heavens, put there by our efforts
Celebrate the day, rejoice in the light from the sun
Swim in the burst of color, from nature surrounding you
Celebrate the day, and all you have to offer
Open up with a positive attitude, and have it return to you
Celebrate the day, so full of life filled with splendor
Jump for joy, to all life has to offer
Celebrate the Day!

Cooking the Different Whole Grains

1 cup brown rice - 2 cups water
Simmer for one hour.
1 cup quinoa - 2 cups water
Simmer for 15 minutes.
1 cup millet – 2 cups water
Simmer for 25 minutes.
1 cup kasha (buckwheat) – 2 cups ware
Simmer for 25 minutes.
1 cup barley – 2 cups water.
Simmer for 30 minutes.
1 cup rolled oats 2 cups water.
Simmer for 30 minutes.
Before cooking, wash the grains, or rinse them whenever possible.

Cheesy Mochi Pasta Casserole

1 lb. elbow pasta – 1 pound firm tofu (crumbled)
1 onion (diced) – 4 cups buttercup squash (small cubes)
    Cook the pasta in boiling water for 10 to 15 minutes, until pasta is soft. Steam the buttercup squash until fork tender. Steam the onion for a couple minutes. In a bowl, mix the pasta, crumbled tofu, onion and squash.
Cheesy Sauce:
2 cups grated Mochi – 2/3 cups tahini – 3/4 cup water
1/3 cup tamari
    Put the sauce ingredients in a sauce pan. Heat on a low temperature until Mochi melts. Pour sauce over the pasta and mix together. Pour into a casserole dish and bake, covered, at 350 degrees for 30 minutes. Uncover and bake an additional 15 minutes.

Kasha Casserole with Tofu Sauce

¾ cup kasha – ¾ cup millet – 3½ cups water
1 onion (diced) – 1 sweet potato (small cubes)
3 garlic cloves (minced)
2 T. tamari – 1 T. tarragon
    Put the water, millet and kasha in a large pot. Bring to a boil. Add the onion, sweet potato and garlic. Cover, reduce heat and simmer for 25 minutes, until all water has been absorbed. Mix in the tamari and tarragon. Place in a casserole dish.
(Continued on next page.)

18

Tofu Sauce:
1 pound firm tofu – 1/4 cup almond butter
3 T. dark miso – 1/2 cup water
  Place sauce ingredients in a food processor. Puree until smooth. Spread over the top of the casserole. Bake at 350 degrees for 20 minutes.

Barley Salad with Creamy Garlic Dressing

1 cup barley – 2½ cups water – 1 cup corn – 1/2 cup peas
1 scallion (thin rounds) – 1 celery stalk (diced)
1/4 cup raisins – 1/4 cup toasted sunflower seeds
  Put the water and barley in a pot. Bring to a boil for a couple minutes. Cover and simmer for 30 minutes, until all water has been absorbed. When barley is done, mix together with the corn, peas, scallion, celery, raisins and sunflower seeds.
Dressing:
½ package (6 oz.) silken tofu – 2 garlic cloves
2 tsp. olive oil – 1 tsp. ume vinegar
½ tsp. ume plum paste – 1 tsp. lemon juice
  To make dressing, put garlic in food processor and chop up very small. Steam the tofu for 5 minutes. Add the tofu, olive oil, ume vinegar, ume paste, and lemon juice to the food processor. Puree until smooth. Pour the dressing over the salad and mix all together. Refrigerate and serve cold.

Pasta with Peanut Butter Sauce

1 pound spaghetti or udon pasta – 1/3 cup raisins
    Cook pasta in boiling water for 10 to 15 minutes until pasta is done.
Sauce:
½ cup peanut butter – ¼ cup rice drink – ¼ cup water
1 T. tamari – ¼ tsp. sea salt – ¼ tsp. turmeric
¼ tsp. cumin
    Put the sauce ingredients in a sauce pan and whisk together as you slowly heat on a low temperature. Once sauce is warm, pour over pasta, add raisins and mix all together. You can serve room temperature or cold.

Brown Rice and Sunflower Seed Salad

1 cup short grain brown rice – 2 cups water
1 cup corn – 2 celery stalks (diced)
2 carrots (diced) – ½ onion (diced)
½ cup toasted sunflower seeds – ¼ cup diced parsley
    Put the brown rice and water in a pot, bring to a boil. Cover, reduce heat to lowest possible temperature, and simmer for one hour. Meanwhile, steam the celery, carrots and onion for a couple minutes until they are al dente, still crisp. Mix together the brown rice, vegetables and sunflower seeds together.
(Continued on next page.)

Dressing:
1 T. olive oil – 2 T. tamari – 1 T. brown rice vinegar
1 T. mirin

Heat dressing on stove, until warm. Pour dressing over salad and mix together. Serve warm or cold.

Nutrition: Sunflower seeds area great source of energy. They give you incredible vitality and help to reduce stress.

Tofu Pasta Salad

1 pound firm tofu – 12 oz. spiral pasta
1/4 onion (diced) – ¼ cup minced parsley

Cook the pasta in boiling water for 10 to 15 minutes, until soft. Steam the tofu for 5 minutes, let cool then crumble the tofu.

Dressing:
2 T. olive oil – 3½ T. tamari – ¼ cup water
1 tsp. thyme – ½ tsp. rosemary – 2 T. brown rice vinegar

Heat dressing until warm. Pour over crumbled tofu, and let marinade for 15 minutes. Mix together the pasta, onion, parsley and marinated tofu. Refrigerate and serve cold.

Quinoa Salad with Walnuts and Raisins

1 cup quinoa – 2 cups water – 2 scallions (sliced thin)
2 carrots (diced small) – 2 celery (diced small)
5 radishes (diced small) – ½ cup raisins
2/3 cup toasted walnuts (chopped)
     Bring the 2 cups water and quinoa to a boil in a pot. Cover, reduce heat to lowest possible temperature, and simmer for 15 minutes, until all water is absorbed. When done, put quinoa in a bowl and let cool.
Dressing:
2 T. olive oil – 4 T. ume vinegar – 4 T. brown rice vinegar
     Whisk together the dressing ingredients. Mix together the quinoa, vegetable, raisins, walnuts and dressing. Refrigerate and serve cold.

Buckwheat Burgers

1 cup short grain brown rice – 2 cups water
½ onion (diced small) – 1 carrot (grated) – 1 cup water
1½ cups buckwheat flour – 2 T. dark miso – 1 T. olive oil
1 tsp. sea salt - 1 tsp. basil – 1 tsp. thyme – 1 tsp. sage
     In a pot, bring the 2 cups water and brown rice to a boil. Cover, reduce to lowest temperature, and simmer for one hour. Put the brown rice and all the rest of the ingredients in a large bowl. Mix together. Form into patties. Place on an oiled cookie sheet. Bake at 350 degrees for 15 minutes. Flip the burgers over and bake another 10 minutes, until they are browned on each side.

Nutrition: Kasha or buckwheat is a gluten-free whole grain that has a wonderful nutty taste. It is a good blood building food, as it neutralizes toxic, acidic wastes. Buckwheat flour is made from unroasted kasha grouts that are ground into flour.

Millet with Mock Cheese Sauce

1½ cups millet – 3½ cups water – 1 onion (diced)
4 garlic (minced) – 3 carrots (diced) – ¼ cup tamari
In a large pot, put the millet, water, onion, garlic and carrots. Bring to a boil, cover, reduce heat to lowest possible temperature and simmer for 25 minutes until all water has been absorbed. When done, add tamari and mix together. Spread the millet in an oiled casserole dish.
Mock Cheese Sauce:
1 pound firm tofu – 2 T. tahini
2 T. lemon juice – 3 T. mellow (light) miso
1 tsp. sea salt – water to blend
Place all sauce ingredients on a food processor. Puree until smooth, adding a little water to create a smooth consistency. Spread the tofu sauce over the millet. Bake at 350 degrees for 30 minutes.
Nutrition: Older than any other grain, millet is the main food of the Hunza people of Asia. High in protein millet is the only grain that is alkaline. Its creamy texture helps relax your middle organs, (spleen, pancreas, stomach) so you can deal with stress more easily.

Macaroni and Mochi

1 pound elbow pasta – 1 cup grated Mochi
1 cup rice drink – ½ cup water – ½ cup tahini
3 T. tamari – 1 tsp. sea salt
     Cook pasta in boiling water for 10 to 15 minutes until soft. In a sauce pan, heat the Mochi, rice drink, water, tahini, tamari and sea salt on a low heat. The Mochi will melt as it heats and create a thick sauce. Once sauce is thick, pour over pasta, mix together. Put in casserole dish, bake, uncovered, at 350 degrees for 30 minutes.
     Cooking tip: My favorite is brown rice pasta. When cooking pasta always start with boiling water. Stir the pasta, occasionally as it cooks so it does not stick together.

Brown Rice and Tempeh Casserole

1 cup short grain brown rice – ¼ cup barley
2½ cups water – 1 (8 oz.) package of tempeh
1 onion (diced) – 2 carrots (diced)
4 garlic cloves (minced) – ½ cup dulse (cut up)
1 tsp. basil – 1 tsp. sage – ½ tsp. thyme –
4 T. dark miso – ½ cup tahini
     Put the brown rice, barley and 2 ½ cups water in a pot. Bring to a boil, add a pinch sea salt, cover, reduce to lowest possible temperature, and simmer for 1 hour. (Continued on next page.)

Crumble the tempeh, put in sauté pan, season with toasted sesame oil and tamari. Brown the tempeh. Place the tempeh in mixing bowl.

Using the same pan, sauté each of the vegetables, one at a time, in toasted sesame oil and tamari. After each vegetable is done, add to the bowl. Add to the bowl, the rice, barley, and rest of ingredients. Using your hands, mix together the casserole to make sure it is well mixed. Put in casserole dish, bake, uncovered, at 350 degrees for 35 minutes.

Nutrition: Tahini is an excellent source of good quality fat, high in protein, and adds a great deal of flavor to your cooking. Tahini is a smooth paste made from sesame seeds. Also high in calcium and iron.

Corn Salad

6 cups corn – 4 celery stalks (diced) – 3 carrots (diced)
2 scallions (sliced thin rounds)
Steam corn until warm, 5 to 7 minutes. Steam the celery, and carrots.
Dressing:
4T. water – 2 T. ume vinegar – 2 T. brown rice vinegar
1 T. olive oil – 2 tsp. tamari – 2 tsp. brown rice syrup
Put dressing ingredients in a pot and warm on stove. Mix together the corn, vegetables and dressing. Serve warm or cold.

<u>Cutting technique:</u> Wrap your hand around the handle of the knife, close to the blade. This ensures leverage so the blade goes through the vegetable easily. Placing your hand further back on the handle makes it more difficult to cut vegetables.

Stir Fried Ginger Brown Rice

4 cups cooked brown rice – 5 scallions (long thin slices)
2 broccoli heads (cut up) – 1 carrot (matchsticks)
5 oz. mushrooms (slices) – 2 cups shredded cabbage
6 inches of ginger (peeled, cut in matchsticks)
toasted sesame oil – tamari

Sauté the ginger in toasted sesame oil and tamari for 2 to 3 minutes. Remove and put in a bowl. Sauté each of the vegetables, one at a time, seasoned with a little toasted sesame oil and tamari. After each vegetable is done add to the bowl. Using the same sauté pan, sauté the brown rice seasoned with toasted sesame oil and tamari. The best way to use the right amount of seasoning is to taste as you are cooking the dish. Once brown rice is done, mix all together and serve.

<u>Nutrition:</u> Ginger contains minerals, calcium, phosphorus, iron, and potassium. It helps stimulate blood circulation and is soothing to an upset stomach. Ginger is a powerful anti-inflammatory food.

Quinoa Salad with a Lemon Twist

1 cup quinoa – 2 cups water – 1 cup peas
2 carrots (diced small) – 1 cup corn
2 scallions (sliced thin) – ¼ cup toasted sunflower seeds
   Put the quinoa and 2 cups water in a pot, bring to a boil. Cover, reduce heat to lowest possible temperature and simmer for 15 minutes. While quinoa is still warm, mix in the vegetables.
Dressing:
2 T. lemon juice – 2 tsp. grated lemon rind
1 T. olive oil – 2 T. ume vinegar – 1 T. brown rice vinegar
   Whisk together the dressing ingredients. Add to the quinoa, add the sunflower seeds, and mix together. Serve warm or chilled.

   Nutrition: Quinoa is a strong plant that flourishes in harsh conditions and gives the body endurance and energy. It is easy to digest and high in lysine, an essential amino acid.

Creamy Almond Pasta Salad

1 pound penne pasta – 2 scallions (sliced thin)
1 carrot (matchsticks) – ½ cup parsley (minced)
    Cook pasta in boiling water for 10 to 15 minutes until soft. Mix pasta and vegetables together.
Dressing:
2/3 cup almond butter – 3 T. tamari – 1/3 cup water
    Whisk together the dressing ingredients. Mix dressing with the pasta salad. Serve warm or cold.
    <u>Nutrition:</u> Don't overlook that piece of parsley on your plate as just garnish. It is also a digestive aid. Bitter to the taste, parsley not only helps stimulate the bowels, it is a blood purifier and anti-carcinogen. And if you have eaten raw garlic or onions, chew on some parsley for fresh breath.

Dijon Pasta Salad

1 pound elbow pasta – 1 onion (diced small)
3 carrots (diced small) – 1 cup corn
3 celery stalks (diced small)
    Cook pasta in boiling water for 10 to 15 minutes, until soft. Steam the vegetables, one at a time, until they are al dente.
(Continued on next page.)

Dressing:
1½ cup Vegenaise – ¾ cup Dijon mustard
3 T. brown rice syrup

Whisk together the dressing ingredients. Mix together the pasta, vegetables and dressing. Refrigerate and serve cold.

Millet Squash Casserole

1 buttercup squash (diced) – 1 onion (diced)
1 tsp. sea salt – 1½ cup millet – 3½ cups water
2 T. tamari - 1 cup grated Mochi – 1½ cups water
additional 2 T. tamari

Put the millet and 3 ½ cups water in a pot, bring to a boil. Cover, reduce heat and simmer for 25 minutes, until all water has been absorbed. When millet is done, mix in 2 T. tamari. Steam the buttercup squash and onion until soft. Put them in a food processor along with the sea salt, puree until smooth. Put the Mochi, 1 ½ cups water, and additional 2 T. tamari in a pot. On a low heat, melt the Mochi. It will thicken as it heats. To put the casserole together, layer first the millet in a casserole dish. Layer the pureed squash mixture on top of millet. Pour Mochi sauce over the top. Bake at 350 degrees for 20 minutes, uncovered.

<u>Cutting technique:</u> Cut onion in half from top to bottom, with the lines. Soak in cold water for 10 minutes. Remove skin, lay flat on cutting board. Going the same direction as the lines, cut straight up and down in wedges. Keep the onion held together with your hand. Now turn the onion and cut across the cuts you just made. The pieces should come out diced.

Wild Rice Pilaf

1½ cup short grain brown rice – ¾ cup wild rice
4 cups water – 4 dried shiitake mushrooms
3 T. tamari – 1 onion (diced) – 3 garlic cloves (minced)
2 carrots (diced) – 2 celery (diced) – 1 tsp. thyme
½ tsp. rosemary – ¼ cup minced parsley

Put the brown rice, wild rice, and 4 cups water in a pot. Bring to a boil. Place the shiitake mushrooms along with the 3 T. tamari in the pot, reduce heat to lowest possible temperature, cover and simmer for one hour. Once rice is done, remove the shiitake mushrooms. Thinly slice the mushrooms, and remove the stem. Discard the stems. Sauté each of the vegetables, one at a time, seasoned with toasted sesame seed oil, and tamari. Mix together the rice, sautéed vegetable, thyme, rosemary, and parsley. Put in a casserole dish. Bake at 350 degrees for 30 minutes.

<u>Nutrition:</u> Not a rice but a seed of a wild aquatic grass, wild rice was a staple of the Native American diet. Wild rice is high in protein and has a fabulous nutty flavor.

~*For Future Generations*~

Experience the world as united
All existing as One
All the fear would become Love
And the pain would be healed
Continue to remember this united feeling
And carry it on
For future generations to come.

Beans

Beans are an excellent source of protein. Protein helps us build and renew muscles, cells and tissues. We need protein in our diet to maintain health. It should come from plant based foods such as beans, to get the benefits of protein without the cholesterol, saturated fat, or toxic nitrogen byproducts. Beans are a power packed food that help strengthen the kidneys and adrenal glands and can help reduce serum cholesterol levels. Beans also contain a photochemical called diosgenin, which appears to inhibit cancer cells from multiplying. Beans and whole grains are partners in a healthy eating plan. They are complementary proteins, one contains the amino acids the other one lacks.

Looking for Stones

Before soaking dried beans, you need to look for stones. Sometimes in the process of packaging, some small stones or clumps of dirt get mixed in with the beans.

Soaking

Dried beans should be soaked before cooking. The larger the bean the longer you need to soak them. Soaking helps eliminate gas and makes the beans more digestible. You should always discard the soaking water.

Kombu

Kombu is a sea vegetable that should always be used when cooking beans. It is high in vitamins minerals, protein, iodine, iron and calcium. But the main reason you cook it with beans is that it strengthens your intestines, thus helping digest the beans and eliminating any gas.

Beans, Tofu
And Tempeh

Tofu and Tempeh

Some of my favorite ingredients to cook with are tofu and tempeh. Both made from the soybean, they are so versatile that the possibilities are endless for these two wondrous foods. Neither one has that much taste by themselves, they take on whatever taste you desire in your recipes. The soybean has been cultivated for about 2,500 years and for good reason. These wonderful beans contain iron, carotene, niacin, vitamins B and B2. They promote clear vision and vitality, as well as improve circulation and support detoxification. Along with all these wonderful traits, soybeans also have isoflavones, which are similar to a natural estrogen that may help prevent hot flashes. They also contain genistein, which helps prevent heart disease and may stop the spread of some cancers in their early stages. These power packed beans also contain protease inhibitors that are a universal anti-carcinogen and may block the action of cancer causing enzymes. And if that is not enough reason to start enjoying these wondrous beans, they also contain phytic acids that inhibit the growth of tumors. You will find the tofu in firm or soft style. The firm is used when you want the tofu to keep its shape, such as marinating it. The soft is better used to create sauces and dressings. Always cook your tofu before eating, cooking makes it more digestible. Tofu is 8% protein, and high in good quality unsaturated fat, 4.3%. It contains all your amino acids and is an excellent source of calcium, iron, phosphorus, potassium, and Vitamins B and E.

The texture of tempeh is chunky, it gives the illusion of meat in some recipes. It is 19.5% protein and it is a complete protein. It contains all the essential amino acids and B12. Tempeh tastes especially good sautéed in toasted sesame oil with a little tamari to season. It can also be crumbled and then molded into patties or loafs.

~Meaningless Things~

Lost in a world of perceptions
Of life and how it should be lived
Keeping track of meaningless things
And losing track of truly important ones.

~Home~

Share the love of all things
Existing here on this planet we call home
Love all creatures
The big and the small
The seen and the unseen
Be grateful for their existence
And honor their lives
Pay homage to the great 'Circle of Life'
That intertwines all our lives
Pay attention to how one effects all
And remember we are not the only ones
Who call this planet 'Home'.

Cooking tip: Recipes that use dried beans can be converted to using canned beans. One, 15 oz. can of beans is equal to ½ cup dried beans. (Example: recipe calls for 1 ½ cups dried beans, you would use, 3 (15 oz.) cans of beans.)

Corny Bean Pie

Bean Filling:
1½ cups black beans – 4 inch piece kombu
½ onion (diced) – 6 garlic cloves (minced)
2 T. dark miso – 2 T. tahini – 1 tsp, sea salt
1 tsp. cumin – 1 cup corn
1 ½ cups cooked brown rice

Soak beans overnight. Discard water. Put beans and kombu in a pressure cooker with enough water to cover. Pressure cook for 15 minutes, drain beans. Put the beans, kombu, onion, garlic, and rest of ingredients in a food processor. Pureed until smooth. Pour in to a bowl and mix in the brown rice.

Crust:
4 T. olive oil – 5 T. water – pinch sea salt
1 cup corn meal – ½ cup oat flour

Mix together the olive oil, sea salt, and water. Add the corn meal and oat flour, mix until you get a firm dough that you can form into a round disc. Wrap in plastic wrap and refrigerate for one hour, until cold. Roll out the crust between two pieces of plastic wrap, and put in an oiled pie pan. Fill the crust with the filling, bake at 350 degrees for 45 minutes.

Black Eyed Peas and Aduki Beans

2 cups black eyed peas – 1 cup aduki beans
1 large onion (diced) – 5 garlic cloves (minced)
4 inch piece kombu – 3 carrots (diced)
2 tsp. cumin – 2 tsp. sea salt – 1½ tsp. thyme

     Soak beans overnight, 6 to 8 hours, you can soak them together because they will be cooked together. Discard soaking water. In a large pot put the kombu, beans, and cover with water. Bring to a boil, reduce heat, cover and simmer for 30 minutes. Add the onions, garlic and carrots. Continue simmer for 20 minutes. Add the cumin, sea salt and thyme. Simmer 5 more minutes, mix together and serve warm.

     Nutrition: Cumin is an aromatic spice that has been used since antiquity. It has a strong pungent taste that gives the impression of a Mexican flavor. It has many health benefits, such as helping assimilate food, improve liver function, and benefiting the digestive system.

Ginger Baked Beans and Squash

4 (15 oz.) cans pinto beans (drain and keep liquid)
1 onion (diced) – organic canola oil and sea salt
4 cups butternut squash (cut in cubes) – 3 T. arrowroot
1½ cup water (use bean liquid) – 1/3 cup dark miso
¼ cup brown rice syrup – 1½ tsp. sea salt
4 tsp. ginger juice (grate fresh ginger and squeeze)

Sauté the onions in canola oil and a pinch sea salt until soft. Steam the squash until fork tender. In a large mixing bowl, put the beans, onion, squash, and arrowroot, mix together. In a sauce pan, put the water, miso, brown rice syrup, and sea salt. Whisk together as it heats on a low temperature. Once warm, turn off heat, and add the ginger juice. Pour sauce over the beans, mix together. Put in a casserole dish, bake at 350 degrees for one hour. Stir every 15 minutes. Serve Warm.

Black Bean Corn Salad

1 cup black beans (soaked 8 to 10 hours)
2 cups elbow brown rice pasta – 1 bay leaf
4 inches kombu – 2 cups corn – 2 scallions (thin slices)
2 carrots (diced) – 1/4 cup minced parsley

Cook the beans, bay leaf, and kombu in a pressure cooker for 15 minutes. Cook pasta in boiling water for 10 to 12 minutes, until soft. Drain beans and mix the pasta, beans and vegetables together. (Continued on next page.)

Dressing:
5 garlic cloves (minced) – 2 T. olive oil
1 T. brown rice syrup – 2 T. brown rice vinegar
4 T. ume vinegar – 2 T. lemon juice – 1 tsp. basil
     Whisk dressing ingredients together, pour over salad and mix together. Refrigerate and serve cold.

Chick Pea and Black Bean Salad

1 cup chick peas – 1 cup black beans
4 inch piece kombu – 4 scallions (thin slices)
3 carrots (diced) – 3 celery (diced)
     Soak the beans overnight, 8 hours. Discard soaking water. Put the beans and kombu in a pressure cooker, add enough water to cover beans, pressure cook for 15 minutes, then drain the beans. Mix the beans and vegetables together.
Dressing:
¼ cup olive oil – 3 garlic cloves (minced)
5 T. brown rice vinegar – 4 T. ume vinegar
     Whisk together the dressing ingredients, pour over salad and mix all together. The longer the dressing marinates over the beans, the better the flavor. Refrigerate and serve cold.
     Cooking tip: Pressure cooking is the quickest and easiest way to cook beans. If you do not have a pressure cooker, you can pot boil the beans. It will take much longer, usually an hour.

Chick Pea Salad

2 cups chick peas – 4 inch piece kombu
2 scallions (thin slices) – 2 broccoli heads (cut up)
4 radishes (thin half-moons)
1 yellow summer squash

      Soak chick peas overnight, 8 to 10 hours. Discard soaking water. Put the chick peas and kombu in pressure cooker, add enough water to cover the beans, pressure cook for 15 minutes. When done, drain the chick peas. Steam the broccoli until fork tender. Mix together the chick peas, broccoli, scallions, radishes and summer squash.

Dressing:
1 T. olive oil – 1/3 cup mirin – ¼ cup tamari
2 tsp. ginger juice (grate fresh ginger and squeeze)

      Put the olive oil, mirin and tamari in a sauce pan, heat until warm. Add the ginger juice. Pour dressing over salad and mix all together. Refrigerate and serve cold.

      <u>Nutrition:</u> Chick peas are also known as garbanzo beans. High in vitamin C and iron, chick peas have a sweet taste and helps support the spleen and pancreas.

Chili Kidney Beans

1½ cups kidney beans (soaked overnight, 8 to 10 hours)
4 inch piece kombu – 1 onion (diced) – 2 carrots (diced)
5 garlic cloves (minced) – 3 celery (diced)
1 small buttercup squash (cut in small cubes)
1 tsp. cumin – 1 tsp. chili powder – 1 ½ tsp. sea salt

Put kombu in bottom of a soup pot. Drain kidney beans and discard water. Place kidney beans in pot. Add just enough water to cover the beans, bring to a boil. Reduce heat, cover and simmer for one hour. Layer the vegetables on top of the beans; onions, carrots, garlic, celery, and squash. Cover and simmer for one more hour. Add spices, mix all together and serve hot.

Kidney Beans and Squash

2 cups kidney beans (soaked overnight, 8 to 10 hours)
2 cups water – 4 inch piece kombu – 1 onion (diced)
1 buttercup squash (cut in cubes small cubes)
1 T. tamari – 2 tsp. sea salt

Bring water to a boil. Add the kombu, then put kidney beans on top. Cover and reduce heat, simmer for 15 minutes. Add the onions, continue simmering for another 15 minutes. Add squash, continue simmering for another 30 minutes. Check to make sure squash is soft, and all water should have been cooked away. Season with tamari and sea salt, mix together and serve warm.

Three Bean Casserole

¾ cup chick peas – ¾ cup black beans
¾ cup kidney beans – 4 inch piece kombu
1 onion (diced) – 5 garlic cloves (minced)
toasted sesame oil, sea salt
½ cup sauerkraut

Soak beans overnight, 8 to 10 hours. Discard water and put beans in a pressure cooker. Cover beans with water, pressure cook for 15 minutes. Drain beans. Sauté the onions in toasted sesame oil and a pinch sea salt until they are starting to brown. Add garlic for the last minute of sautéing. Mix beans, sauerkraut and vegetables together and put in a casserole dish.

Sauce:
1½ cups water – ¼ cup yellow mustard
¼ cup tahini – 2 T. dark miso
2 T. arrowroot – 1 tsp. sea salt

Whisk together sauce ingredients in a sauce pan, heat on low, whisk occasionally. Sauce will thicken as it heats. Pour sauce over beans, bake at 350 degrees, uncovered for 30 minutes. Serve warm.

Cooking tip: When cooking beans with the kombu, you can leave kombu in the dish. When you pressure cook the kombu it becomes so soft it just falls apart and you can mix in to whatever dish you are creating.

Cutting board care: Before you start cutting vegetables, wet your wooden cutting board. This will prevent the wood from absorbing the color and odor of whatever you are cutting. Wooden cutting boards are my favorite, they are more natural. If properly cared for they will last a long time. Avoid using any soap on your wood, it will dry out the wood. Once a year, oil your cutting board with some natural oil.

Tempeh Goulash

1 lb. brown rice elbow pasta – 8 oz. tempeh
olive oil – tamari
1 onion (diced) – 1 tsp. thyme – 1 tsp. basil
½ tsp. paprika – ½ tsp. cumin
2 cups grated Mochi – ¼ cup tahini
¼ cup tamari – ½ cup water

Cook pasta in boiling water for 10 minutes until soft. Crumble tempeh, put in sauté pan, add a little olive oil and tamari and start to brown tempeh. Add the onion, thyme, basil, paprika and cumin. Sauté for about 7 minutes until onion is soft. In a mixing bowl, put the pasta, sautéed tempeh and onions, grated Mochi, tahini, tamari, and water, Mix all together and put in a casserole dish. Bake at 350 degrees, covered, for 30 minutes. Uncover, bake an additional 10 minutes. Serve hot.

Tofu Fries

1 lb. firm tofu – organic canola oil
Marinade:
1/3 cup tamari – 2 T. water - 2 T. olive oil
1 T. brown rice syrup – ½ tsp. sea salt
Flour Dredge:
3 T. oat flour – 3 T. arrowroot

    Cut the tofu in rectangle logs, to resemble the shape of french fries. Whisk marinade ingredients together. Put tofu in a shallow dish, pour marinade over and let marinade for 30 minutes. Heat a large amount of canola oil in a pot, about 2 inches deep. Oil should be about 325 degrees. Mix the oat flour and arrowroot together. Roll each piece of tofu in the batter. In batches of 5 or 6 pieces, fry the tofu until it is browned and batter is crispy. Remove from oil, place on paper towel, to absorb extra oil, Sprinkle sea salt over tofu while hot, serve and enjoy.

    Dip the tofu fries in Val's Ranch Dressing in the Tofu Lettuce Salad with Ranch Dressing, page 81.

Cheesy Tempeh

16 oz. tempeh (crumbled) – toasted sesame oil – tamari
2 onions (thin half-moons) – 4 carrots (thin rounds

    Sauté the crumbled tempeh in toasted sesame oil and tamari until browned. Remove from pan, put in a casserole dish. Using the same pan, sauté the onions in toasted sesame oil and tamari until browned. Add onions to tempeh and using same pan, sauté the carrot the same way and add to casserole.

Cheesy Sauce:
1 cup grated Mochi – ¾ cup water
¼ cup tahini – 2 T. dark miso

    Whisk together the sauce ingredients in a sauce pan as it slowly heats on a low temperature. Sauce will thicken as Mochi melts. Once sauce is thick, pour over casserole, cover, and bake at 350 degrees for 30 minutes. Uncover and bake an additional 10 minutes. Serve warm.

Tofu Sausage

1 lb. firm tofu – ½ onion – 3 garlic cloves – 2 T. tamari
1 T. dark miso – 2 T. tahini – ¼ cup olive oil
2 T. brown rice syrup – ½ tsp. sea salt – 1 tsp. rosemary
1 tsp. sage – ½ tsp. fennel – ½ tsp. thyme
½ tsp. paprika – 1 cup oat flour – canola oil
corn meal grits (optional)

Put the onions and garlic in food processor, chop up very small. Add the rest of the ingredients, (except the oat flour and corn meal grits) to the food processor and puree until smooth. Put batter in bowl and mix in the oat flour. Refrigerate until cold. Form into patties. You can coat the patties with the corn meal, if you desire a bit of crunch on the outside of sausage, or you can cook without the corn meal coating. Heat about 1/4 inch of canola oil in a sauté pan. Brown the patties on each side.

Corny Tofu Patties

1 lb. firm tofu – 3 T. tamari – ½ onion
½ cup corn – 1 carrot (grated) – 2 T. minced parsley
5 white mushrooms (diced small) – ½ tsp. sea salt
¼ cup dulse (soaked and cut up) – ½ tsp. paprika
¼ tsp. curry – 1 ½ cup corn meal grits
½ cup water – canola oil
(Continued on next page.)

Crumble the tofu and marinate in the 3 T. tamari for 30 minutes. Sauté the onions in canola oil and sea salt until soft. Using the same pan, sauté the mushrooms and carrots in canola oil and sea salt, until soft. Put in a bowl, tofu, and sautéed vegetable. Add the rest of ingredients; parsley, sea salt, dulse, paprika, curry, corn meal grits, and water (use the dulse soaking water), mix all together. Form into patties. Heat canola oil in sauté pan, brown the patties on each side.

Tofu Mock Chicken Salad

1½ lb. firm tofu – ¼ cup tamari
¼ cup toasted sesame oil – ¼ onion (diced)
4 celery stalks (diced)
Cut the tofu in ¼ inch slices, place in shallow dish and marinate for 30 minutes, in the ¼ cup tamari and toasted sesame oil. Place tofu on a cookie sheet, bake at 350 degrees for 25 minutes. You can save and use marinate for another time. After tofu has baked, let it cool and cut in to small cubes. Mix together in a bowl the tofu, onions, and celery.
Dressing:
2 cups Vegenaise – 2 T. dill pickle relish
4 tsp. stone ground mustard
Whisk together the dressing ingredients, and mix in the salad. Refrigerate and serve cold.

Tempeh Burgers

8 oz. tempeh – ¼ onion (minced) – 1 garlic (minced)
2 T. tamari – 1 T. dulse (cut up) – 1 T. tahini
1/3 cup walnuts (ground up) – ½ tsp. basil
¼ tsp. sage – ¼ cup oat flour – 2 T. water

Crumble the tempeh. Mix all the ingredients together. Form into patties, heat some canola oil in a sauté pan, and brown the patties on each side. Serve on a whole grain bun. These patties freeze very well.

Nutrition: Dulse is a purple-reddish sea vegetable, both delicious and nutritious. It is 25% protein and a good source of Vitamin C, E and B complex. This tasty sea vegetable can be used in a wide variety of ways including sautéing, as a condiment or in a casserole. A great source of iodine and iron, but what truly makes it unique is that you can eat it right out of the bag.

Portobello and Tempeh

8 oz. tempeh – toasted sesame oil – tamari
6 oz. Portobello mushroom slices
¼ tsp. cumin – ¼ tsp. curry – brown rice vinegar

Brown the tempeh, whole, in toasted sesame oil and tamari. Cut in to cubes. Using the same pan, sauté the mushrooms in toasted sesame oil and tamari for about 5 minutes until soft. Cut the mushrooms in to same size pieces as tempeh. (Continued on next page.)

Put the mushrooms and tempeh back in pan, add spices, and continue to sauté for a couple minutes. Turn off heat, sprinkle a little brown rice vinegar over the dish. Serve warm.

Cooking tip: When buying brown rice vinegar, look for, traditionally fermented or brewed vinegar, this insures it was made in the time honored tradition of natural fermentation. It has a sweet, pungent, sour, flavor that complement the other flavors in many dishes.

Aduki Bean Salad

1 cup aduki beans – 4 inch piece kombu
2 cups water – ½ onion (diced)
1 zucchini (diced) – 1 carrot (diced)
Soak aduki beans for 6 hours. Discard soaking water. Put in a pot, the beans, kombu, and 2 cups water, bring to a boil, reduce heat, cover and simmer for one hour, until soft. Drains the beans and let cool.
Dressing:
¼ cup water – 1 T. dark miso
1 T. barley malt – 1 tsp. sea salt
Whisk together the dressing, pour over the beans and vegetables and mix all together. Refrigerate and serve cold.

Shopping tip: These small red beans can be spelled differently; aduki, azduki, azuki, are all the same beans.

Mexican Refried Beans

2 (15 oz.) cans pinto beans – 1 onion (diced)
4 garlic cloves (minced) – 2 tsp. tamari
2 tsp. sea salt – 1 tsp. cumin
1 tsp. Mexican seasoning (or chili powder)
     Sauté the onion in olive oil and a pinch of sea salt until soft. Add garlic and continue sautéing for a minute. Drain one can of beans, and do not drain one can, put in food processor. Add the tamari, sea salt, cumin and Mexican seasoning, puree until smooth. Add the beans to the sauté pan. Heat and stir occasionally for 10 minutes. Great as a chip dip, or in burritos.

~Opportunities~

*Blind people read, but do not see
Deaf people talk, but do not hear
Life grants us opportunities
That we do not take
Fear holds us hostage
Love sets us free.*

Vegetables

Vegetables

Always remember, 'variety is the spice of life'. When it comes to vegetables, use a wide variety. Experiment with all different kinds. Next time you go to the grocery store, buy a different kind of vegetable that you have never tried before. Bring it home, first try it raw to see what it tastes like, than experiment with it. Try steaming, pot boiling, sautéing it, or put it in a soup. Have fun with your vegetables.

Besides fresh vegetables, also experiment with sea vegetables. Probably the most nutritious food on the planet, they are packed full of vitamins, minerals, trace minerals, calcium (11 to 14 times more than milk), iron, and folic acid. They also can help cleanse toxic metals out of your system, and even radiation. They have the ability to reduce blood pressure, and have anti-tumor and antibiotic properties. Bitter to the taste, you only need a little bit to go a long way, but that little bit can be very beneficial.

Don't forget your leafy green vegetables. They are rich in chlorophyll, iron, calcium, and an excellent source of vitamins C. These dark green vegetables are packed full of protein.

It is important to have a sharp knife when cutting vegetables frequently. You are more likely to cut yourself with a dull knife from it slipping off the vegetable, than from a sharp one that will cut through with ease. Have fun with the wide variety of colorful vegetables Mother Nature has so generously provided for us.

~What paves the Universal Road~

Happy thoughts are what paves
The Universal Road of your 'Souls' journey.

~I Love the Night~

I love the night, its darkness covers me
Like a familiar blanket, of comfort from my kin
I love the night, all the stars shinning
Millions of little worlds as vast
As the imagination can conceive
I love the night, the bright moon
Silhouetted in the darkness
So full of power, it demands your attention
I love the night, the still quietness
That reminds you of where you came from
And where you know you will go back to.

Kale Chips

1 bunch kale (cut up in pieces, stem removed)
Olive oil, sea salt

Put kale in a bowl. Drizzle olive oil over kale. Mix olive oil through the kale with your hands. Spread the kale on a couple cookie sheets, single layer. Sprinkle sea salt over kale. Bake at 350 degrees for 7 minutes until kale is crisp.

Kale and Corn Sauté

7 kale leaves (cut up) – 1 cup corn
1 onion (thin half-moons) – 2 T. tamari – 2 T. water
1 T. mirin – 1 T. lemon juice – 1 T. toasted sesame seeds

Sauté the onion in toasted sesame oil and a dash of tamari for 5 minutes. Place kale on top of onion and corn on top of the kale. Add tamari, water, Mirin, and lemon juice. Cover and simmer for 10 minutes. Uncover, add the sesame seeds, mix all together and serve.

Mushrooms in Garlic Sauce

5 cups mushrooms (cut in half) – 6 garlic cloves (minced)
4 T. olive oil – ½ tsp. sea salt – 1 T. lemon juice
1 T. minced parsley

Sauté the garlic in olive oil for 5 minutes. Add the mushrooms to the sauté. (Continued on next page.)

Cover and cook for 5 minutes. Uncover and add sea salt. Sauté for a couple more minutes. Remove from heat, add lemon juice and parsley. Mix together and serve warm.

Nutrition: Garlic stimulates metabolism and is used to treat both chronic and acute diseases. It has been used for medicinal purposes for thousands of years. It helps stabilize blood sugar levels and has anti-bacterial, anti-carcinogenic, and anti-fungal properties.

Baked Stuffed Onions

2 large onions (cut ends off, cut in half through middle)
1 cup cooked brown rice – 2 T. pine nuts
¼ tsp. thyme – toasted sesame oil – tamari

Scoop out some of the middle of the onion and mince it. Sauté the minced onion in toasted sesame oil and tamari until it starts to brown. Now add pine nuts, thyme and brown rice. Sprinkle some tamari over for taste. Stuff the onion halves with the stuffing. Place in a casserole dish. Pour in some water (1/2 inch in depth), cover and bake for 30 minutes at 350 degrees. Uncover and serve warm.

Kale Catalina

1 bunch kale (cut up) – 1/3 cup pine nuts
6 garlic cloves (minced) – 1/3 cup raisins – 2 T. olive oil
1 T. tamari – 2 T. lemon juice – ¼ cup water

     In a large sauté pan, sauté the garlic in olive oil for 2 minutes. Remove garlic and oil, set aside for later. Put the raisins in the sauté pan, then put the kale on top of raisins. Add the ¼ cup water, cover and cook for 7 minutes. Put the olive oil and garlic back in pan. Continue cooking for another 5 minutes. Add the lemon juice and pine nuts. Stir together and serve warm.

     <u>Cutting technique:</u> When cooking with garlic, first remove the skin. Do this by placing a clove on your cutting board. Put your knife flat on the clove and give it a little whack with the palm of your hand. The skin should peel off the clove with ease. Cut off the dried tip of the clove. To mince the garlic keep cutting it into little pieces until it is in very small pieces.

Creamy Vegetables

½ lb. brussels sprouts (cut in half)
1 onion (thin half-moons) – ½ head cauliflower (cut up)
1 (6 inch) piece daikon (cut in cubes)
½ head cabbage (diced) – 2 cups grated Mochi

(Continued on next page.)

Bring a pot of water to a boil. Quick boil each vegetable, one at a time in the boiling water. Place all vegetables and Mochi in a casserole dish and mix together. White Sauce:

1½ cup rice drink – ¾ cup water – 2 T. olive oil
2 tsp. sea salt – ¾ cup oat flour – 1 T. tamari

Put the rice drink, water, olive oil, tamari, and sea salt in a pot. On a low heat, slowly start to heat the sauce up. Whisk in the flour. Continue to heat and whisk occasionally. As it heats the sauce will thicken. Pour the thickened white sauce over the vegetables in casserole dish. Bake, covered, for 40 minutes at 350 degrees. Uncover and bake an additional 10 minutes. Serve warm.

Arame Sauté

1 onion (half moons) – 3 garlic cloves (minced)
1 cup arame – 2 carrots (matchsticks)
1 broccoli head (cut up) – 1 cup cabbage (diced)
1 cup mushrooms (sliced) – 4 T. sunflower seeds
¼ cup water – 4 T. tamari – 3 T. mirin

Sauté the onions in toasted sesame oil and a dash of tamari for about 5 minutes. Wash the arame by swishing in around in a bowl full of water, and drain. Place arame on top of onions. Layer the rest of the vegetables, garlic, carrots, broccoli, cabbage, and mushrooms on top of arame. Add 2 T. tamari and 1 T. mirin and ¼ cup water. Cover and simmer for 20 minutes. Mix in the remaining 2 T. tamari, 1 T. mirin and sunflower seeds. Serve warm.

Baked Vegetables

1 onion (cut in half moons) – 2 turnips (cubed)
1 (6 inch piece) daikon (cubed) – 1 broccoli head (cut up)
½ buttercup squash (cut in cubes) – 1/3 cup olive oil
1/3 cup tamari – 1/3 cup water – 1 tsp. sea salt
2 cups grated Mochi

     Place all vegetables in a casserole dish. Mix together the olive oil, tamari, water and sea salt. Pour over vegetables. Cover and bake at 350 degrees for 45 minutes, stirring every 15 minutes. Uncover, stir in Mochi and bake an additional 15 minutes.

     <u>Nutrition:</u> Mochi is made from sweet brown rice that has been steamed and pounded, it looks like a square block. It is high in fiber, calcium and iron. Mochi can help with blood sugar imbalances, for people with anemia, and helps strengthen intestines. When grated and then cooked it becomes sticky and gives the illusion of cheese.

Mixed Greens Stir Fry

½ onion (half moons) – 1 carrot (matchsticks)
3 collard green leaves (cut up)
1 cup chopped daikon greens
1 cup carrot greens – 1 T. lemon juice
2 tsp. mirin – 2 T. sunflower seeds
tamari – olive oil
(Continued on next page.)

Sauté the onions in olive oil and a dash of tamari until they turn translucent. Add the carrots, a little more olive oil and dash of tamari and sauté for a couple minutes. Add the greens, sprinkle a dash of tamari over greens, and add the lemon juice and mirin. Cover and steam vegetables for a couple minutes. Remove lid, add sunflower seeds, mix all together and serve right away.

Nutrition: Daikon is in the radish family. It is a long white root and when you get it fresh, the greens should still be attached. The greens help aid in digestion and contains diuretic properties.

Squash Rings

1 winter squash (acorn, butternut, delicate, or buttercup)
olive oil – tamari

Cut squash in thin round slices. Remove seeds form the middle. Mix equal amounts of olive oil and tamari in a shallow bowl. Dip both sides of squash rings into mixture and place on a cookie sheet. Bake at 350 degrees for 10 minutes on each side, 20 minutes total. Serve warm or cold for a snack.

Nutrition: Indigenous to the Americans, squash has a wonderful sweet taste that helps nurture the spleen, pancreas, and stomach. High in vitamin A and C, potassium and magnesium, and squash also helps build your immune system.

Marinated Portobello Mushrooms

8 oz. sliced Portobello mushrooms
Marinade:
1 T. olive oil – 4 T. tamari
4 T. brown rice vinegar – 4 T. water
2 garlic cloves (minced)

Place mushrooms in a shallow dish, Mix together the marinade, and pour over mushrooms. Let sit 30 minutes. Heat sauté pan, place mushrooms in the pan. Brown on each side. Serve warm.

Nutrition: High in vitamin E, olive oil is the only oil that can be truly cold pressed. An excellent source of good quality monounsaturated fat.

Tamari Almond Green Beans

2 cups green beans – 1/3 cup sliced almonds
Toasted sesame oil – tamari

Lightly steam the green beans. Heat a small amount of toasted sesame oil in a sauté pan. Sauté the almonds, seasoned with a little tamari, for a couple minutes. Add the Green beans, season with a little more tamari. Sauté until dish is heated. Taste and adjust seasoning.

Nutrition: Green beans have an ample supply of calcium, potassium and vitamin A and B complex.

Broccoli and Arame

1 onion (thin half moons) – 3 broccoli heads (cut up)
2 carrots (matchsticks) – ½ cup arame
¼ cup tahini – 1 T. ume plum paste – 1 cup water
1/3 cup minced parsley (for garnish)

Sauté the onions in toasted sesame oil and a pinch of sea salt, until soft. Wash the arame by swishing it in a bowl and draining. Put the arame over the onions. Layer the carrots and broccoli on top of the arame. Mix the tahini, ume paste, and water together, and pour 2/3 of the mixture over the dish. Cover and simmer for 10 minutes. Add the remaining liquid. Continue simmering, covered for 10 more minutes. Mix in parsley and serve.

Nutrition: High in calcium, arame is sold, dried and shredded. As it cooks it will expand, a little bit goes a long way. Used medicinally for female problems, it supports hormone functions. It is high in protein, Vitamin A, B complex and naturally occurring iodine.

Sweet and Sour Kale

1 bunch kale (cut in small pieces) – 1 cup sauerkraut
1 apple (cut in thin slices) – ½ tsp. sea salt – 1 cup water

Place apple, water and sea salt in a pot. Bring to a boil, then cook for about 3 minutes. Add kale, cover and cook for 7 minutes. Now add sauerkraut, continue to cook, covered for 10 minutes. Mix all together and serve.

Cauliflower Au Gratin

1 large head cauliflower – 2 cups grated Mochi
5 T. tahini – 2 T. tamari – 2 T. ume plum vinegar
2 T. water

Bring water to a boil in a large pot. Put the whole head of cauliflower in the pot and boil for 10 minutes, or until cauliflower is soft. Remove cauliflower and place in a casserole dish. Mix together the Mochi, tahini, tamari, ume vinegar, and water. Using your hands, coat the cauliflower head with the Mochi mixture. Cover the whole head. Bake at 350 degrees for 20 minutes.

Nutrition: With its large white head, the cauliflower appears to resemble the brain. Because of this, it is considered excellent food for your brain by many cultures. High in vitamin C, fiber, riboflavin, magnesium, and sweet to the taste, it belongs to the cabbage family.

Garlic Roasted Turnips

4 turnips (cut in small cubes) – 5 garlic cloves (minced)
¼ cup olive oil – 1 tsp. sea salt - chopped parsley

Mix everything together in a casserole dish. Cover and bake at 350 degrees for 45 minutes. Uncover, and continue to bake for another 15 minutes. Serve with chopped parsley for garnish.

Cooking tip: Turnips are in the cabbage family, they have an amazing sweet taste when roasted.

Layered Vegetable Wakame Casserole

1½ onions (sliced thin) – 8 inches wakame
1½ sweet potato (peeled and sliced thin
8 garlic cloves (minced) – 6 cups kale (cut up)
Sauce:
½ cup rice drink – 2 T. tamari – 1 T. olive oil
1 T. brown rice vinegar – ½ tsp. sea salt

     Spread the onions on a single layer in a casserole dish. Soak the wakame for 4 minutes, until soft. Cut in small pieces, layer over the onions. Layer the sliced sweet potato next, then garlic and kale on top. Whisk together the sauce ingredients, and pour over the casserole. Bake at 350 degrees for 50 minutes. Uncover and bake an additional 5 minutes and serve warm.

Deep Fried Brussels Sprouts

Organic canola oil – brussels sprouts (cut in half)
brown rice vinegar – sea salt

     Heat a large amount of canola oil in a deep pan to deep fry the brussels sprouts. Heat the oil to 325 degrees, Place the brussels sprouts in the hot oil. Be careful because the sprouts will make the oil splatter. Fry the sprouts until they are well done, almost blackened. Remove from oil, put in bowl, sprinkle brown rice vinegar and sea salt over the sprouts and mix to cover with the seasoning. Eat hot.

~Beautiful Clouds~

Forming beautiful clouds in my mind
Of fluffy bunnies
And puffy sheep
Of angels flying around
And smiling faces
Peering at me from above
Of castles floating in the sky
And horses trotting by
Of mountains taller than the trees
And flying birds of all shapes and sizes
Seeing them all from
The eyes inside my soul.

~I Am Not Alone~

God had blessed me with so many gifts
Too numerous to count
The sun that warms my heart
The breeze that sweeps me away
The animals that live only to be loved
The beautiful trees that give me strength
The bright moon that illuminates my soul
All these blessings remind me that
I am not alone.

Soups and Salads

Soups

Soup, the ultimate comfort food. Easy to prepare, soups serve an important part in a healthy lifestyle. You can start any meal with a small cup, or have it as the main dish. When creating a soup, start with boiling water or soup stock. Add one vegetable at a time, starting with a sweet vegetable, such as onions, to create a sweet broth. Before adding your next vegetable, always wait until the water comes back up to a boil. This enhances the flavor, locking in the individual flavors of each vegetables, so your onions taste like onions, and your carrots taste like carrots. When using miso, always add it at the end of cooking and never boil the miso. Miso has enzymes and amino acids that can be destroyed by boiling. By cutting your vegetables differently, you can create soups for the different seasons. In the winter, cut your vegetables in bigger pieces so they will absorb more heat and create more warmth in your body. Then, in the summer months, cut the vegetables smaller so they don't absorb as much heat.

Salads

Salads are a refreshing addition to your meals on a hot summer day. Try to get dark, leafy lettuces for your salad. The darker the lettuce, the more nutrients it contains. Pressed salads area type of fermented salad. To make them, you may want to get a pickle press. You can find them at health food stores or search the internet for one.

Pressed salads and naturally fermented pickles consist of three things; salt, pressure and time. This is the way our ancestors stored food for the winter months. Everyone's ancestors ate naturally fermented foods, and for good reason. Fermented foods strengthen your intestines, and provide enzymes that aid in digestion. These digestive aids also help keep the flora in the intestines healthy and produce lactic acid in the colon.

~*Pure Joy*~

Watching a cat walk through the grass
Walking through the woods
Feeling the breeze through my hair
Hearing the sounds of silence
Smelling the air just after it rains
Sleeping outside under the stars
Laughing so hard you cry
Crying so hard you laugh
Seeing the face of your child
Remembering your favorite moment
Keeping faith in your heart
Creating abundance for others
Displaying true love
Experiencing the Oneness.

Millet Chili

2 cups kidney beans (picked over and soaked overnight)*
4 inch piece kombu – 3 cups water – 1 cup millet
8 cups water – 2 onions (diced) – 8 garlic cloves (minced)
6 celery stalks (diced) – 2 tsp. cumin – 2 tsp. chili powder
2 tsp. sea salt – 1 T. ume plum paste – 1/3 cup dark miso
     Pressure cook the kidney beans and kombu in the 3 cups water for 15 minutes. Meanwhile, bring the 8 cups water to a boil. Rinse the millet and add to the boiling water. Cook for 5 minutes. Add the onions and garlic, cover, and simmer for 15 minutes. Add the cooked kidney beans, water and kombu. (The kombu softened as it cooks and will fall apart.) Add celery, continue to simmer, covered for 15 minutes. Turn heat off. Take some of the hot broth and dissolve the ume plum paste and miso in the broth. Pour back in chili. Add cumin, chili powder and sea salt. Mix all together, let sit 5 minutes before serving.
    *You can substitute 4 (15 oz.) cans of cooked beans for the 2 cups dried beans.
    Cutting technique: When holding a vegetable to cut, curl your fingers in. You should be holding the vegetable with just tips of your fingers. You are less likely to cut yourself this way. And always lay the vegetables flat side down on the cutting board creating a stable cutting surface.

Squash Soup

9 cups water – 1 onion (diced) – ½ acorn squash
½ dumpling squash – ½ buttercup squash
¼ cup dark miso – 2 T. tahini – 1 tsp. sea salt

    Cut the squashes in to small cubes. Bring water to a boil in a soup pot. Add onions, and squashes, one at a time. Let the water come back up to a boil in between each one. Reduce to a simmer, cover and simmer for 15 minutes. Take some of the hot broth and dissolve the miso, tahini and sea salt, and pour back in soup. Mix, and serve.

Aduki Bean Soup

1½ cups aduki beans (picked over and soaked 6 hours)
8 cups water – 4 inch piece kombu (soaked, cut small)
1 onion (diced) – 3 carrots (thin rounds)
18 inches burdock root (thin rounds) – 1 ½ tsp. cumin
2 T. mirin – 4 T. light miso – 1 tsp. sea salt
1 T. grated ginger, juiced

    Bring water to a boil in a soup pot. Add aduki beans and kombu. Cover, simmer for 45 minutes. Add onions, carrots and burdock. Cover and simmer for 20 more minutes. Dissolve miso in some of the hot broth. Add the rest of the seasonings, mix, and serve.

    Nutrition: Burdock root helps cleanse the blood, supports digestion and eliminate toxins. Containing inulin, burdock is good for diabetic conditions, also contains; protein, calcium, phosphorus and potassium.

Creamy Mushroom Soup

6 cups water – 2 cups rice drink – 2 cups rolled oats
1 onion (diced) – 6 cups chopped mushrooms
6 garlic cloves (chopped) – ¼ cup light miso
¼ cup tahini – 1½ tsp. sea salt
   Bring the water and rice drink to a boil in a soup pot. Add rolled oats, onion, mushroom and garlic. Cover, reduce to a simmer for 20 minutes. Add the miso, tahini and sea salt. Using a hand blender or food processor, puree soup until you get a thick creamy soup. Serve hot.

French Onion Soup

12 cups water – 2 T. olive oil – 9 T. tamari – 1 tsp. sea salt
1 tsp. basil – 3 large onions (thin half moons)
   In a soup pot, sauté the onions in olive oil and a dash on tamari for 10 to 15 minutes, until the onions are soft. Add the water and bring to a boil. Reduce to a simmer, add the 9 T. tamari, sea salt and basil, cover, simmer for 15 minutes. Serve hot.
   <u>Nutrition:</u> Tamari is the healthy version of soy sauce. Made from naturally fermented soybeans, it is a salty, wheat-free condiment. Known for its rich taste, it contains living enzymes that help with the secretion of digestive liquids.

Yellow Split Pea Soup

10 cups water – 2 cups yellow split peas
3 T. barley – 4 inch piece kombu (soaked, cut up)
1 onion (diced) – 5 garlic cloves (minced)
3 carrots (diced) – 3 celery stalks (diced)
2 cups corn – 4 T. tamari – 1 T. olive oil
1 tsp. sea salt – 1 tsp. marjoram
½ tsp. thyme – ½ tsp. rosemary

Bring water to a boil in a soup pot. Add the split peas, barley and kombu. Reduce heat, cover and simmer for 20 minutes. Add the onion, garlic, carrots, and celery, cover and simmer for another 45 minutes, until the split peas have dissolved and the soup is thick. Add the seasoning, mix and serve hot.

Nutrition: Yellow split peas are an ancient legume that has been around since prehistoric times, it is high in protein. Split peas dissipate when they cook to create a thick soup. The yellow split pea has a sweet, nutty flavor. It is a main staple in the European diet.

Chick Pea Soup

1½ cups chick peas (picked over, soaked overnight)*
4 inch piece kombu – 10 cups water – 1 onion (diced)
4 garlic cloves (minced) – 2 carrots (diced)
2 celery (diced) – 1 small buttercup squash (small cubes)
2 cups corn – 3 T. tamari – 1½ tsp. oregano
1 tsp. basil – ½ tsp. rosemary – 2 tsp. sea salt

Put chick peas and kombu in a pressure cooker, cover with water, pressure cook for 15 minutes. Strain the chick peas and use the water as part of the 10 cups to make soup. Kombu will have fallen apart in the cooking process, you can just add it to the soup. Bring the 10 cups of water to a boil, add the vegetables, one at a time, letting the water come back up to a boil between each one. Cover, reduce heat and simmer for 15 minutes. Add the chick peas, continue to simmer for 10 more minutes. Add corn, tamari and rest of seasonings. Mix and serve warm.

*You can substitute 3 (15 oz.) cans of cooked chick peas for 1½ cups dried chick peas. Strain the canned beans use the liquid for the 10 cups water, and then skip the pressure cooking of the beans.

Cooking tip: When creating a dish, always chop your vegetables in relatively the same size. If you have all different sizes, the big pieces will be under cooked and the small pieces will be over cooked.

White Water Chili

1 cup kidney beans – 1 cup white beans – 6 cups water
4 inch piece kombu – 2 cups rice drink – 2 onions (diced)
6 garlic cloves (minced) – 4 celery stalks (diced)
¼ cup dark miso – 1 T. ume plum paste – 1 tsp. cumin
1 tsp. chili powder – 1 tsp. paprika – 1 tsp. sea salt

Pick over the beans, and soak overnight. Discard the soaking water. Bring the 6 cups water and rice drink to a boil in a soup pot. Add the beans and kombu, bring to a boil, reduce heat, cover and simmer for 30 minutes. Add the onions, garlic and celery, Continue to simmer for 30 more minutes. Take some of the hot broth, dissolve the miso and ump plum paste in broth, add back to pot. Add the seasonings, mix and serve warm.

Lentil Soup

9 cups water – 2 cup red lentils – 4 inch piece kombu
1 onion (diced) – 4 garlic cloves (minced)
3 carrots (half-moons) – 3 celery (diced) – 2 cups corn
3 tsp. sea salt – 1 tsp. cumin – 1 tsp. turmeric

Bring the 9 cups water to a boil in a soup pot. Pick through the lentils. Add the lentils and kombu to pot. Cover, reduce heat and simmer for 10 minutes. Add the onions, garlic, carrots and celery, simmer for 20 minutes. Add corn and seasonings, mix and serve warm.

Tofu Miso Soup

8 cups water – 1 onion (thin half moons) – tamari
toasted sesame oil - 8 inches wakame (soaked and cut up)
1 lb. firm tofu - 4 dried shiitake mushrooms – 1 cup corn
2 carrots (matchsticks) - 1/3 cup dark miso
¼ cup minced parsley – ½ tsp. sea salt

Soak the shiitake mushrooms for 15 minutes until soft. Use the soaking water as part of the 8 cups water. Cut shiitakes in thin slices. Sauté the onions and carrots in a little toasted sesame oil and tamari in a large soup pot until vegetables are soft. Add the 8 cups water, bring to a boil, add wakame and shiitake mushrooms. Cover, reduce heat, and simmer for 15 minutes. Cut tofu in small cubes, add to soup, and simmer for 10 minutes. Take some of the hot broth and dissolve the miso in broth, add back to pot along with the corn and sea salt. Mix in parsley, serve warm.

Nutrition: Shiitake mushrooms are powerful, medicinal mushrooms, they add wonderful flavor to your soup. Use the dried ones for a stronger flavor. Drying the mushrooms enhances the flavor and medicinal properties. Shiitakes are known for their anti-viral and anti-tumor properties.

Creamy Carrot Soup

4 cups water – 2 cups rice drink – 5 large carrots (cut up)
½ onion (cut up) – 1 cup rolled oats – 1½ tsp. sea salt
1½ tsp. ume plum vinegar – 1½ tsp. ume plum paste
Put the water, rice drink, carrots, onions, rolled oats, in a soup pot and bring to a boil. Cover, reduce heat, and simmer for 20 minutes. Add sea salt, ume vinegar and paste, then puree soup. Using either a hand lender, food processor, or blender, blend until its smooth and creamy.
Soup imitates tomato soup without the tomatoes.

Delicata Bisque

2 delicata squash – 2 cups rice drink – 2 cups water
1 onion (chopped) – 1 cup cooked brown rice
1 tsp. sea salt
Cut delicata squash in half, length wise. Lay flat on a cookie sheet, bake for 45 minutes at 350 degrees until fork tender. Scoop out and discard the seeds, scoop out the flesh and save. Bring the rice drink and water up to a boil in a soup pot. Add onions, squash, and cooked brown rice, cover, and simmer for 25 minutes. Add sea salt and blend, using either a hand blender, food processor or blender. Blend until you get a thick, creamy soup, serve warm.
Cooking tip: Delicata is one of the sweetest winter squashes, it is a small, oblong, narrow, yellow with green strips.

Cream of Broccoli and Mushroom Soup

8 cups water – 2 cups rice drink – 1 onion (chopped)
4 cups chopped broccoli – 2 cups chopped mushrooms
1½ cups rolled oats - 4 garlic cloves (chopped)   1
T. olive oil – 3 tsp. sea salt
    Bring water and rice drink to a boil in a soup pot. Add vegetables, rolled oats and garlic, bring soup back up to a boil. Reduce heat, cover and simmer for 20 minutes. Add olive oil and sea salt, blend soup using either a hand blender, food processor or blender. Serve warm.

Lentil and Asparagus Soup

9 cups water – 4 inch piece kombu – 2 cups red lentils
1 onion (diced) – 6 garlic cloves (minced)
2 carrots (diced) – 1 lb. asparagus (1/2 inch pieces)
¼ cup light miso – ½ tsp. sea salt
1 tsp. sage – 1 tsp. dried basil
    Bring water to a boil in a soup pot. Add the kombu, cook for a couple minutes until kombu is soft. Remove kombu, cut in small pieces, add back to the soup pot. Add the lentils and bring back up to a boil. Add the vegetables, one at a time, letting the water come back up to a boil in between each one. Reduce heat to low, cover and simmer for 20 minutes. Dissolve the miso and sea salt in hot soup broth, pour back in soup, add spices, mix, and serve hot.

Colorful Salad with Creamy Garlic Dressing

1 bunch red leaf lettuce (washed, small pieces)
1 cucumber (1/4 moons) – ¼ purple onion (diced)
1 yellow summer squash (matchsticks)
1 carrot (matchsticks) – 2 T. raisins
Dressing:
1 package organic silken, firm tofu – 2 garlic cloves
1 T. olive oil – 1 T. brown rice vinegar – 2 T. mirin
1 tsp. ume plum paste – 1 tsp. ume plum vinegar

In a large bowl, toss together the vegetables, salad ingredients. Steam the tofu for 3 to 4 minutes. Put garlic cloves in food processor and mince. Add the tofu and rest of the dressing ingredients to food processor, puree until smooth. Serve the salad with dressing poured over top.

Yellow and Green Salad

2 yellow summer squash (1/4 moons) – olive oil
2 zucchini (1/4 moons) – sea salt – ½ tsp. basil
3 tsp. tamari – 2 tsp. brown rice vinegar
2 tsp. brown rice syrup – pinch sea salt

Sauté the yellow squash in olive oil and pinch of sea salt for 2 to 3 minutes, put in a bowl. Using the same pan, sauté the zucchini the same way, add to bowl. Mix in the basil. Heat the rest of the ingredients until warm. Pour over salad and mix together. Serve warm or cold.

Quick Cucumber Pickles

1 cucumber (sliced thin) – 3 tsp. ume plum vinegar
3 tsp. brown rice vinegar

     Place cucumbers in a shallow dish. Pour ume plum vinegar and brown rice vinegar over cucumbers. Let sit for 1 to 3 hours, mix together and serve.

Sweet Pressed Salad

¼ head cabbage (shredded) – ½ cucumber (thin slices)
5 Napa summer cabbage leaves (shredded)
½ apple (sliced thin) – 3 T. raisins
1 carrot (matchsticks) – 1 ½ tsp. sea salt

     Place all vegetables and raisins in a large bowl. Sprinkle sea salt over the vegetables, mix together using your hands, gently squeezing the vegetables as you mix. The natural juices from the vegetable will start to come out. Place salad in a pickle press and press them. If you do not have a pickle press, put salad in a large jar of bowl, and place something heavy on top to create pressure. Let sit on counter for 24 hours, then refrigerate. Serve cold.

     <u>Nutrition:</u> Napa cabbage: Sweeter, juicer, crisper and tenderer than traditional cabbage, Napa cabbage is sometimes called Chinese or summer cabbage. It is very low in calories and sodium. It is an excellent source of vitamin A.

Red and Green Pressed Salad

¼ head purple cabbage (shredded) - 4 radish (sliced thin)
¼ head Napa summer cabbage (shredded)
1 cucumber (sliced thin) – 1 garlic clove (minced)
4 tsp. ume plum vinegar
Dressing:
2 T. tamari – 2 T. tahini – 3 T. brown rice vinegar
¼ cup water – 2 tsp. dried parsley
    Mix all vegetables together with ume plum vinegar.
Place in pickle press and press for one hour. Whisk
together the dressing ingredients. To serve, squeeze excess
water out of salad, pour dressing over salad.

Pressed Salad with Wakame

6 cups Napa summer cabbage (shredded)
½ head radicchio (shredded) – 1 carrot (matchsticks)
1 cucumber (sliced thin) – 4 radish (sliced thin)
½ cup raisins - 2 T. ume plum vinegar – ½ tsp. sea salt
12 inches wakame – 2 T. brown rice vinegar
    Using your hands and gently squeezing, mix all the
vegetable (except wakame) with ume plum vinegar and sea
salt. Place in pickle press, press for 10 to 12 hours.
Marinade the wakame in 2 T. brown rice vinegar for 30
minutes. Mix the salad with the wakame plus marinade,
squeeze the liquid out of the salad and place on plate.

Summer Dulse Salad with Rosemary Dressing

1/3 lb. mixed salad greens – watercress (garnish)
½ head radicchio (cut up) – 2 scallions (thin slices)
½ cup dulse (cut up)
Dressing:
2 T. toasted sesame oil – 2 T. tamari – 2 T. water
2 T. brown rice vinegar – 1 T. mirin – 1 tsp. rosemary
2 T. toasted sesame seeds

    Toss the lettuce, radicchio, scallions and dulse together in a salad bowl. Place the dressing ingredients in a pan and heat on stove until warm. Let dressing cool, pour over salad and garnish with a little chopped watercress.

Kidney Bean and Beet Salad

1/3 lb. mixed salad greens – 2 small beets
1 (15 oz.) can kidney beans (drained)
1 yellow summer squash (matchsticks)
2 scallions (thin slices) – 1 cucumber (1/4 moons)
1 T. dulse flakes – toasted sunflower seeds
Dressing:
2 T. tamari – 4 T. olive oil – 2 pinches sea salt

    Wash beets, cover beets with water in a pot, boil for 20 minutes until fork tender. Let beets cool, peel beets, skin will come right off after boiling, slice beets. Arrange salad greens on plate, top with rest of salad ingredients. Warm dressing on stove, let cool, serve over salad.

Tempeh Peanut Salad with Ranch Dressing

8 oz. tempeh – toasted sesame oil – tamari
1 bunch red leaf lettuce – 1 carrot (grated)
¼ onion (diced) – 1 cucumber (1/4 moons)
1 T. dulse flakes – ¼ cup peanuts
  Cut tempeh in 12 equal slices. Brown both sides of the tempeh slices in toasted sesame oil and tamari. Cut in small squares. Cut up the red lettuce, mix in a bowl along with the carrot, onion, cucumber, dulse flakes and peanuts. Place tempeh on top, drizzle, Ranch Dressing over salad.

Ranch Dressing

1 cup Vegenaise (vegan mayonnaise) – 1 T. lemon juice
1 T. brown rice vinegar – 2 tsp. tarragon
2 tsp. ume plum vinegar
  Put all ingredients in a bowl and whisk together. Serve with the Tempeh Salad, Tofu Lettuce Salad and with the Tofu Fries.

Tofu Lettuce Salad with Ranch Dressing

1 lb. firm tofu (crumbled) – 1 T. olive oil – 1 tsp. tamari
1 tsp. ume plum vinegar – ½ tsp. sea salt – ¼ tsp. turmeric
½ onion (diced) – mixed salad greens – 1 T. dulse flakes
Crumbled organic corn chips

Sauté the onion in the 1 T. olive oil, and pinch sea salt for a couple minutes. Add the crumbled tofu, tamari, ume vinegar, sea salt and turmeric. Sauté for 7 minutes, until all is cooked. Arrange salad greens on a plate, top with sauté tofu, dulse flakes, and crumbled corn chips. Drizzle, Ranch Dressing over top.

Sweet Potato Salad

2 large sweet potatoes (peeled, cut in cubes)
1 lb. firm tofu (crumbled) – 1 T. olive oil – 1 tsp. sea salt
¼ tsp. tamari – ½ onion (diced) – 2 celery stalks (diced)
1¼ cup Vegenaise (vegan mayonnaise)
¼ cup yellow mustard

Boil the sweet potatoes for 7-10 minutes, until fork tender, drain and cool. Sauté the tofu in the olive oil, sea salt and tamari, 7 minutes, let cool. Mix together the sweet potatoes, tofu, onion, celery, Vegenaise and yellow mustard. Serve cold.

This is my most popular recipe, it tastes like traditional potato salad, using sweet potatoes for a healthier version.

Breakfast
and
Beverages

Breakfast and Beverages

Breakfast is the most important meal of the day. What to do now that you have decided to live a healthy lifestyle? Most of the time, I have soup for breakfast. This may seem like a foreign idea to some, but our ancestors ate soup, and gruel for breakfast for centuries. Your breakfast soup can contain, whole grains, beans, and a wide variety of vegetables. Eating whole grains, beans and vegetables in the morning will give you energy throughout the day.

Toast and Bread

Look for bread with the least amount of ingredients, and without white flour. Sour dough bread made with a fermented starter (a fermented mixture of flour and water) is one of the oldest forms of bread and one of the most delicious. Sprouted grain breads are good for those who have difficulties digesting flour products.

Beverages

Sweet beverages in the morning can help satisfy that sweet craving, and using Amazake as the sweetener will not spike your blood sugar. Amazake, is a sweet, fermented drink made from brown rice. The Amazake sweet drinks in this section also make a great evening, relaxing drink.

~The Light~

Oh, the Light surrounds me
It glows so brilliant, radiant and true
I will attract more Light
And more Light will show
Then darkness sometimes will appear
If I fight the darkness, it will expand and grow
But to meet the ugly face with Love and Light
It will disappear with no trace
Then the Light that surrounds me will expand and grow
More bright then anyone can know.

~Song of Love~

Sing a song of Love and it comes back to you
The song will show you the way
All the beauty that surrounds you
Came from the song you sang today
Sing a song of Love and the birds join in
The trees dance to the tune
Your heart leaps as the flowers bloom
Sing a song of Love and the whole world
Will sing with you.

Cinnamon Rolls

½ cup Amazake – 1/3 cup olive oil – 2 T. tahini
¼ cup apple juice – 2 T. baking powder – pinch sea salt
2½ cups whole grain flour (whole wheat, oat, brown rice)
     Put Amazake, olive oil, tahini, apple juice and sea salt in food processor, puree until smooth. Pour mixture into a bowl, stir in the flour and baking powder. Form into a large flat disc, wrap in plastic wrap and refrigerate for an hour. Place dough in between two pieces of plastic wrap, and roll out dough. Make the dough in the shape of a large rectangle, about 1/3 inch thick.

Filling:
3 T. raisins – 3 T. olive oil – 2 T. pecans (chopped)
½ cup brown rice syrup – 2 tsp. dark miso
Pinch sea salt – cinnamon – allspice
     Put raisins, olive oil, pecans, brown rice syrup, miso and sea salt in a food processor and puree. Pour the filling over the dough rectangle, and spread out evenly. Sprinkle a generous amount of cinnamon over the filling and sprinkle a little allspice over the cinnamon. Take the edge of the dough and start to roll the dough to form a large log. Cut the log in approx. 2 inch thick pieces. Place in an oiled casserole dish, one right next to each other. Bake at 350 degrees for 40 minutes. Heat some brown rice syrup in a pan and brush over rolls.
     These cinnamon rolls are non-yeasted.

Maple Pecan Bread

2 T. flax seed meal – ¼ cup vanilla pecan Amazake
½ cup water – ¼ cup olive oil – ½ cup maple syrup
1 tsp. brown rice vinegar – 1 tsp. vanilla – ¼ tsp. sea salt
2 tsp. baking powder – 1 tsp. cinnamon - pinch allspice
2 cups whole grain flour (wheat, oat, brown rice)
1 cup chopped pecans

Put flax seed meal and water in a food processor, puree until frothy. Add Amazake, oil, maple syrup, brown rice vinegar, vanilla, sea salt, baking powder, cinnamon and allspice, puree until smooth. Shift flour in to a mixing bowl, add the wet ingredients, and mix all together. Pour in to an oiled bread pan, bake at 350 degrees for 40 minutes.

You can make muffins with this recipe. Bake for 30 minutes in a muffin pan.

Millet Carrot Muffins

¼ cup olive oil – 2 cups cooked millet – ¾ cup water
1 cup shredded carrot – ¼ cup lemon juice – pinch sea salt
1 cup rolled oats – 1 cup oat flour – ½ cup raisins

Mix together the oil, millet, lemon juice, water and sea salt. Mix in the shredded carrots, rolled oats, and oat flour, add the raisins last. Scoop in to an oiled muffin pan, bake at 350 degrees for 35 minutes.

Nutrition: Rolled oats are high in fiber, they can help stabilize blood sugar and help reduce high cholesterol.

Cinnamon Raisin French Toast

1 loaf cinnamon raisin whole grain bread – 2 T. olive oil
1½ cups rice drink – 2 tsp. egg replacer – pinch cinnamon
 Whisk the egg replacer in the rice drink. Mix together with the oil and cinnamon, pour in to a shallow dish. Dip a slice of the bread, quickly, in to the mixture, and put on a heated, oiled griddle. Cook for approx. 7 minutes, until it is browned, flip over and cook for another 5 minutes.
Cinnamon Syrup:
½ cup brown rice syrup – ¼ cup maple syrup
1 tsp. cinnamon – pinch sea salt
 Whisk together the ingredients in a sauce pan, heat on stove for 5 minutes. Serve hot over french toast.

Cranberry Raisin Muffins

¼ cup olive oil – ¼ cup brown rice syrup – ½ cup water
½ cup apple juice – 1 tsp. cinnamon – ¼ tsp. nutmeg
¼ tsp. allspice – pinch sea salt – 1 T. baking powder
2½ cups whole grain flour (wheat, oat, brown rice)
½ cup cranberries – ¼ cup raisins – ¼ cup chopped pecans
 Whisk together the oil, brown rice syrup, water, apple juice, cinnamon, nutmeg, allspice sea salt and baking powder. Shift the flour in to a mixing bowl.
(Continued on next page.)

Mix the wet ingredients with the flour. Fold in the cranberries, raisins and pecan. Scoop in to an oiled muffin pan, bake at 350 degrees for 30 minutes.

Cooking tip: Whole grain flours have all the fiber, vitamins and mineral still in them. If you wish to make gluten-free baked goods, I recommend oat flour. It has a nice lightness, and moisture content to create a nice texture.

Scrambled Tofu (Mock Eggs)

1 lb. fresh, firm tofu – 1 T. olive oil – ¼ tsp. turmeric
1 tsp. ume plum vinegar – ½ tsp. tamari – ½ tsp. sea salt
½ onion (diced) – 1 carrot (diced) – 1/2 cup peas
½ cup chopped mushrooms

Crumble tofu, put in sauté pan, add oil, turmeric, vinegar, tamari and sea salt. Mix all together and cook for about 7 minutes until starting to brown. Remove from pan, and put in a bowl. Using the same pan, sauté the vegetables in a little olive oil and pinch sea salt. Add to bowl and mix all together. Serve warm.

Hot Brown Rice Cereal

1½ cup cooked brown rice – 1 cup rice drink
1 tsp. cinnamon – ¼ tsp. allspice – pinch sea salt
¼ cup raisins – 1/4 cup chopped walnuts
    Put all ingredients in a sauce pan. Simmer for 10 minutes. Serve hot and enjoy!
    <u>Cooking tip:</u> Rice drink is my favorite for taste and texture. Made from brown rice, vegetable oils and sea salt. You can use your favorite non-dairy drink for this recipe.

Millet Browns
(Tastes like hash browns)

1 cup millet – 2½ cups water – ½ onion (diced)
4 T. rice drink – 4 T. olive oil – 2 T. arrowroot
1 tsp. sea salt
    Put the millet, water and onion in a pot, bring to a boil. Reduce heat, cover, and simmer for 20 minutes. Put millet in mixing bowl, add rest of ingredients, and mix everything together. Heat some olive oil in a skillet, form the mixture in to small patties, put in skillet. Brown the patties on one side, flip over, brown on the other side.

Breakfast Energy Soup

10 cups water – 1 onion (diced) – 1 rutabaga (diced)
8 inches wakame (soaked and cut up) – 2 carrots (diced)
4 cups buttercup squash (cubes) – 1 zucchini (diced)
1 cup minced kale – 4 cups cooked brown rice
1 (15 oz.) can aduki beans (or your favorite beans)
1/3 cup dark miso – 1 tsp. sea salt

Bring water to a boil in a large soup pot. Add the vegetables one at a time, letting water come back up to a boil in between each vegetable. Once all vegetables are in soup pot, cover, reduce to low temperature, and simmer for 15 minutes. Drain the beans, add them along with the brown rice to the soup, and continue simmering for another 10 minutes. Turn off heat, dissolve the miso and sea salt in some hot broth, add back to the soup pot, and mix together. Serve hot.

The Perfect Oatmeal

1 cup rolled oats – 2 cups water – pinch sea salt
¼ cup Amazake – ½ tsp. cinnamon – pinch allspice
1/3 cup raisins – 1/3 cup chopped walnuts

Place all ingredients in a pot. Bring to a boil. Reduce heat to low, cover and simmer for 25 minutes. Serve hot with a little rice drink.

Roma Cappuccino

¾ cup rice drink – ¼ cup Amazake – pinch cinnamon
2 tsp. Roma (coffee substitute)

Heat the rice drink, Amazake, and Roma until it boils. Put in blender and blend until frothy. Pour in mug, sprinkle cinnamon over top, and serve hot.

Cooking tip: Roma is a coffee substitute made from roasted malted barley, roasted barley, chicory and rye. You can get all the full body, bitter taste of coffee, without all the caffeine.

Relaxing Tea

¼ onion (diced small) – ¼ cup carrots (diced small)
¼ cup buttercup squash (diced small)
¼ cup cabbage (diced small) – 4 cups water

Bring water to a boil, add the vegetables. Reduce heat to low, simmer for 20 minutes. Strain the tea, discard the vegetables (all their flavor is now in the tea). Drink tea warm.

The sweet taste from cooking these vegetables nurtures your spleen, pancreas and stomach. By nurturing these organs you are able to relax and not be so uptight.

Rice Tea

4 cups water – ½ cup brown rice – pinch sea salt

Rinse brown rice, and put in a dry heated skillet or sauté pan. Dry roast the brown rice for 10 minutes, stirring occasionally, until it starts to smell fragrant and turns yellow. Put the roasted brown rice in a pot along with the 4 cups water and pinch sea salt. Bring to a boil, reduce heat, and simmer for 30 minutes. Pour the tea through a strainer and discard the rice. (Rice is not cooked all the way after only 30 minutes.) Serve the tea warm or room temperature.

An excellent tea for summer time, it can help normalize the body's temperature.

Hot Chocolate
(One serving)

½ cup Amazake – ½ cup rice drink – 1 tsp. baking cocoa

Put all ingredients in a pot. Whisk together as it starts to heat, bring to a boil. For a frothy hot chocolate, put in blender before serving.

Nutrition: Amazake is made from fermented sweet brown rice, this sweet drink resembles the taste of a thick malt. It is an ideal sweetener because it increases blood sugar slowly rather than rapidly, such as white sugar does. It is nutrient dense and easily digested.

Dairy Free Mock Chocolate Milk
(One serving)

¼ cup Amazake – 1 cup rice drink
1 tsp. Roma (coffee substitute)

Put Roma in cup, pour Amazake and rice drink in cup, whisk until thoroughly mixed. It takes a couple minutes for Roma to completely dissolve. The Roma imparts a chocolate taste. Serve cold.

<u>Nutrition:</u> Chocolate is considered very yin, and not advised on a healing diet for certain conditions. This recipe can be a substitute for anyone eliminating chocolate from their diets.

~*The World As One*~

See the world as one, and you will heal it
See the world as one, and you will not harm it
See the world as one, and you won't judge it
See the world as one, and you won't criticize it
See the world as one, and you won't blame it
See the world as one, or you won't see it at all.

Desserts

Desserts

There is nothing as satisfying as creating the perfect dessert. It seems to please everyone. Desserts are maybe my favorite thing to make and I have spent much of my time perfecting them. In the beginning of my healthy journey, my desserts gave me some grief. I can't tell you how many times I made a cake and no matter how long it baked, it never solidified in the middle. Or how many pies I threw out because I couldn't roll out the crust and the inside was like soup. It take some practice and knowledge of the secrets of using different ingredients, so don't give up. To help, I will share all the secrets I have learned along the way.

Making the Perfect Pie

When making the crust, make sure all the ingredients are cold. After mixing the dough together, wrap in plastic wrap and refrigerate. Roll the dough out in between two pieces of plastic wrap, wax paper or parchment paper. This helps so you can easily correct the shape of the crust without it sticking to your rolling pin.

The filling of pies holds together better if you cook the filling in a sauce pan first before baking in oven.

Making the Perfect Cake

A good egg replacer for cakes is the combination of brown rice vinegar and baking powder. Flaxseed meal and water, pureed together, creates a frothy mixture that can also be used as an egg replacer.

~The Song~

Hear the song of peace that calms the soul
Hear the song of love that fills you with bright light
Hear the song of freedom where you feel eternity
Hear the song of nature that resonates with the Oneness
Hear the song of gratitude that brings your hearts desire
Hear the song of your soul that tells you, you are home.

~God's Presence~

The trees call to me and I hear their pleas
'Oh, please come and play'
The beauty of the sun as it shines on their leaves
Takes my breath away
I see so much beauty in nature
And I stand in gratitude to Thee
Here in the woods you need no reminder
For Your presence is all around
And no one can take that away.

Chocolate Cake
(Two Layer Cake)

Wet:
½ cup olive oil – 1 cup brown rice syrup
½ cup maple syrup – 1 T. brown rice vinegar
¾ cup rice drink – 1 T. vanilla – pinch sea salt
Dry:
3½ cups whole grain flour (oat, barley, whole wheat)
1 T. baking powder – 1 ½ tsp. arrowroot
¾ cup unsweetened baking cocoa
    Put wet ingredients in a food processor or blender, puree until smooth. Sift the baking cocoa and flour in to a mixing bowl. Add baking powder and arrowroot. Pour the wet ingredients in to the bowl and mix together. Pour batter into 2 nine inch oiled cake pans. Bake at 350 degrees for 35 minutes.

Fudge Frosting
(Frosts a Two Layer Cake)

¾ cup rice drink – 4 T. agar flakes – pinch sea salt
½ cup brown rice syrup – 1/3 cup tahini
1½ cup grain sweetened chocolate chips
½ cup Amazake
(Continued on next page.)

Simmer agar flakes, rice drink, brown rice syrup and sea salt, for 7 minutes. Add tahini and chocolate chips, whisk together as the chips melt. Stirring constantly, warm for 4 minutes. Cool in refrigerator for 2 hours. While cold, put in food processor, add the ½ cup Amazake and puree until smooth, frost the cake.

Mocha Coffee Cake with Pecan Glaze

Wet:
2 T. Roma (coffee substitute) – 1 T. flax seed meal
2/3 cup rice drink – ½ cup brown rice syrup
¼ cup olive oil – 2 T. maple syrup – ¼ tsp. sea salt
1 tsp. brown rice vinegar
Dry:
2 cups whole grain flour (oat, spelt, barley)
1 T. Roma (coffee substitute) – 2 tsp. baking powder
         Put the flax seed meal and rice drink in blender or food processor. Blend until frothy. Add rest of wet ingredients and blend. Mix together the dry ingredients in a bowl. Add the wet to the dry and mix all together. Pour into an oiled 9 inch, round cake pan, bake at 350 degrees for 25 minutes.
Pecan Glaze:
¼ cup Amazake – ¼ cup rice drink – 1/3 cup pecans
         Place ingredients in a sauce pan. Heat until it boils. Remove from heat and let cool. Once cake and glaze have cooled, pour glaze over cake.

Carrot Cake
(Two Layer Cake)

Wet:
½ cup olive oil – ¾ cup brown rice syrup
¼ cup maple syrup – ¾ cup rice drink
1 T. brown rice vinegar – ¼ tsp. sea salt
Dry:
3 cups whole grain flour (oat, spelt, barley)
2 T. baking powder – 1 T. cinnamon – 1 tsp. cloves
½ tsp. ginger – 3 cups grated carrots
¾ cup raisins – ½ cup chopped walnuts

    Whisk together the wet ingredients. Mix the dry ingredients together in separate bowl. Mix the wet with the dry ingredients. Pour into two, oiled, 9 inch, round cake pans, bake at 350 degrees for 40 minutes. Let cool before frosting.

Tofu Cream Frosting

1 (12 oz.) package silken, firm tofu
½ cup brown rice syrup - 1 T. maple syrup
1 T. lemon juice – ¼ tsp. sea salt – ¼ cup arrowroot

    Puree ingredients in a food processor, puree until smooth. Heat in a sauce pan on low heat, until it starts to thicken. Refrigerate for a couple hours, until cold. Frost cake and store in refrigerator.

Mexican Spice Cake
(One Layer Cake)

Wet:
¼ cup olive oil – 3 T. maple syrup – 2 T. barley malt*
2 T. brown rice syrup – ¼ cup rice drink
1 tsp. brown rice vinegar – ¼ tsp. sea salt
Dry:
1¾ cup whole grain flour (oat, spelt, barley)
1 tsp. cinnamon – 1 tsp. baking powder – 1 tsp. arrowroot
½ tsp. cardamom – ½ tsp. coriander – ¼ tsp. cloves
½ cup raisins

 Whisk together the wet ingredients. Mix together the dry ingredients in a separate bowl. Mix the wet and dry ingredients together. Pour batter into a 9 inch, round, oiled cake pan. Bake at 350 degrees for 30 minutes. Cake is so flavorful you do not need frosting, but if you desire one, frost with the Tofu Cream Frosting after cake has cooled.

 *For a gluten-free cake, substitute brown rice syrup for the 2 T. barley malt.

Cherry Pie

Crust:
½ cup olive oil – ½ cup water – ¼ tsp. sea salt
3 cups whole grain flour (oat, spelt, barley)
Filling:
5 cups dark sweet cherries – ¾ cup brown rice syrup
1 cup pecans (chopped) – ¼ cup water
¼ cup arrowroot – ¼ tsp. sea salt

Whisk together the olive oil, ½ cup water and ¼ tsp. sea salt. Mix in the flour until you have a stiff dough that holds together. Divide the dough in half, form each half in to a flat, round disc. Wrap in plastic wrap and refrigerate until cold. Place one of the dough discs in between two pieces of plastic wrap and roll out. Put in an oiled pie pan.

Place all filling ingredient in a sauce pan, heat on low. As the filling heats up, start to stir, it will thicken as it heats. Once filling is heated and thick, pour into crust. Roll out the top crust, and place over pie. Bake at 350 degrees for one hour. Let cool completely before cutting.

Cooking tip: To make gluten-free desserts, I use oat flour. It has a light consistency, natural flavor, and creates moist, delicious desserts.

Blueberry Apple Pie

Pressed Crust:
1 cup walnuts – 1 ½ cup brown rice flour – ¼ cup olive oil
¼ cup brown rice syrup – ¼ cup water
1 tsp. cinnamon – pinch sea salt
Filling:
4 cups apples (peeled and cut up) – 2 cups blueberries
½ cup brown rice syrup – ¼ cup water – 5 T. arrowroot
2 tsp. cinnamon – 1 tsp. ginger – ¼ tsp. sea salt

    To make crust, mix together the water, brown rice syrup, olive oil, cinnamon and sea salt. Put walnuts in a food processor and finely chop them. Mix in the walnuts and flour. Wet your hands, press ¾ of the dough in to an oiled pie pan. Put the filling ingredients in a sauce pan, on a low heat, covered, slowly heat the filling until it starts to thicken, stirring a couple times as it heats. Pour the filling into the pie crust, crumble the remaining crust dough over the top of pie. Bake at 350 degrees for 45 minutes. Let cool completely before cutting.

Tofu Cream Pie with Cookie Crumb Crust

Crust:
1½ cup cookie crumbs – 2 T. olive oil – 2 T. apple juice
Filling:
1 (12 oz.) package silken firm tofu
½ cup brown rice syrup
2 T. maple syrup – 1 T. tahini – 2 tsp. vanilla
1 T. lemon juice – 3 T. arrowroot – pinch sea salt

Mix the crust ingredients together. Press in to an oiled pie pan. Put all the filling ingredients in a food processor, puree until smooth. Pour into the pie crust, bake at 350 degrees for 50 minutes. Let cool completely, refrigerate, serve cold.

Cooking tip: Put cookies in food processor and chop the cookies up until you have crumbs. The Ginger Snap Cookies (page 109) make great cookie crumbs.

Fruit Topping for Pie

1 cup your favorite fruit (blueberries, raspberries)
1/3 cup brown rice syrup – 2 T. arrowroot – pinch sea salt

Put all ingredient in a sauce pan, on low heat, slowly heat on stove. Stir a couple times as it heats, once thick, pour over Tofu Cream Pie.

Apple Pie

Crust:
3 cups whole grain flour (spelt, oat, brown rice)
½ cup olive oil – ½ cup water – 1 T. brown rice syrup
1 tsp. cinnamon – 1 tsp. ginger – ¼ tsp. sea salt
Filling:
8 cups apples (peeled and cut up)
½ cup brown rice syrup – ½ cup water – 4 T. arrowroot
1 T. dark miso* – 1 tsp. cinnamon – ½ tsp. ginger

To prepare crust, mix together the olive oil, water, brown rice syrup, cinnamon, ginger and sea salt. Mix in the flour, you should get at firm dough that you can form into a ball. Divide the dough in half, form each half in to a round flat disc, wrap in plastic wrap, refrigerate until cold. Place one disc of cold dough in between two pieces of plastic wrap and roll out dough, put into an oiled pie pan. Whisk together the brown rice syrup, water, arrowroot, miso, cinnamon and ginger, mix with the apples. Put all in a sauce pan, on low heat, slowly heat on stove, it will thicken as it heat. Once it has started to thicken, turn off heat, pour in to the bottom pie crust. Roll out the top crust the same way, place over the pie. Pinch the sides together, poke a couple holes in the top of pie. Bake at 350 degrees for one hour. Let cool completely before cutting.

*I use miso in this recipe in place of sea salt. The dark, rich flavor of the miso complements taste in the pie.

Pecan Pie

Crust:
¼ cup olive oil – ¼ cup water – pinch sea salt
1½ cups whole grain flour (spelt, oat, brown rice)
Caramelized Topping:
2/3 cup brown rice syrup – 1/3 cup barley malt*
¼ cup Amazake – ¼ cup rice drink – pinch sea salt
1 cup pecans – pinch allspice
Creamy Middle:
½ cup Amazake – ½ cup brown rice syrup – pinch sea salt
½ cup rice drink – 2 cups pecans – 3 T. arrowroot

Mix together the olive oil, water, sea salt and whole grain flour. The dough should stick together, form into a round flat disc, wrap in plastic wrap and refrigerate until cold. Roll out the dough in between two pieces of plastic wrap, place in an oiled pie pan. Put all the caramelized topping ingredients in a sauce pan and bring to a boil. Reduce to low, simmer for 10 minutes. Place all of the creamy middle ingredients in a food processor and puree until you have a thick creamy texture. Spread the creamy middle into the pie crust. Gently, pour the caramelized topping over the top. Bake at 350 degrees for 45 minutes. Let cool completely before cutting.

This is one of my favorite holiday pies I make it every year for my family's Thanksgiving dinner. (Pictured on page 96.)

*Substitute brown rice syrup for barley malt to make gluten free.

Blueberry Pear Pie with Cinnamon Raisin Crust

Crust:
½ cup olive oil – ½ cup water – 1/3 cup raisins
2 tsp. cinnamon – ¼ tsp. sea salt
3 cups whole grain flour (spelt, oat, brown rice)
Filling:
2 pears (diced) – 2 cups blueberries – 2 T. lemon juice
½ cup brown rice syrup – ¼ cup barley malt*
¼ cup arrow root – pinch sea salt

To make crust, put the olive oil, water, raisins, cinnamon and ¼ tsp. sea salt in a food processor and puree. Mix together the pureed mixture and flour, you should get a dough that sticks together. Divide the dough into two equal pieces, form a flat round disc, wrap in plastic crap and refrigerate until cold. Roll out one of the discs between two pieces of plastic wrap. Place in an oiled pie pan. Place all of the filling ingredient in a sauce pan, on low heat slowly heat until starting to become thick. Stir a couple times while heating. Pour the filling into the bottom crust. Roll out the top crust, put on top, pinch the sides, and poke a few small holes in the top of pie. Bake at 350 degrees for 45 minutes. Let cool completely before cutting.

*You can substitute all brown rice syrup in place of the barley malt for a gluten-free pie.

Cookie Pizza

Crust:
¼ cup olive oil – ½ cup brown rice syrup – 1 tsp. vanilla
1 T. tahini – 2 T. water – 2 T. arrowroot – ¼ tsp. sea salt
2¼ cup whole grain flour (spelt, oat, brown rice)
Peanut Butter Sauce:
¾ cup peanut butter – ½ cup brown rice syrup
Toppings:
½ cup grain sweetened chocolate chips – coconut
½ cup raisins

To make crust, whisk together the olive oil, brown rice syrup, vanilla, tahini, water and sea salt. Mix in the arrowroot and flour, you should get a firm dough. Form into a large flat disc. Wrap in plastic wrap, refrigerate until cold. Roll out in between two pieces of plastic wrap, about ¼ inch thick, and round to look like a pizza. Place on an oiled cookie sheet or pizza pan, curl up the edges of the dough to form a lip. Bake at 350 degrees for 15 minutes. Mix the peanut butter and brown rice syrup together. Spread on the crust while crust is warm. Sprinkle the chocolate chips and raisins over the top. Garnish with a little coconut, put back in oven for 10 minutes. Cut while still hot. Serve warm or room temperature.

You could use a variety of different toppings for this recipe, your favorite chopped nuts, or dried fruit.

Peanut Butter Cookies

1¼ cup peanut butter – 1/3 cup olive oil – 1 tsp. vanilla
1 cup brown rice syrup – ¼ cup water – pinch sea salt
2¼ cup whole grain flour (spelt, oat, brown rice)

Put in a food processor the peanut butter, olive oil, vanilla, brown rice syrup, water and sea salt. Puree until smooth. Mix together the pureed mixture with the flour. Spoon on to an oiled cookie sheet, press down with a fork. Bake at 350 degrees for 15 minutes, let cool before eating,

Ginger Snap Cookies

1/3 cup olive oil – ¾ cup brown rice syrup – pinch sea salt
½ cup rice drink – 1 tsp. ginger – 1 tsp. cinnamon
¼ tsp. cloves – ¼ tsp. allspice
4½ cup whole grain flour (spelt, oat, brown rice)

Put in a food processor the olive oil, brown rice syrup, sea salt, rice drink, ginger, cinnamon, cloves and allspice, puree until smooth. Mix pureed mixture with the flour. Spoon onto an oiled cookie sheet. Bake at 350 degrees for 15 minutes. Let cool before eating.

These make great cookie crumbs. Put cookies in a food processor, chop until you have fine cookie crumbs.

~The Big Chocolate Chip Cookie~

The big chocolate chip cookie
Is waiting for you enjoyment
It is cooling from the oven, ripe full of chips
Made with love and affection, full of untamed flavor
Just right for your tired taste buds
To get a shocking 'Jolt'
Out of their hum-drum life.

Giant Mocha Chocolate Chip Cookies

1/3 cup olive oil – 2/3 cup brown rice syrup
1 T. flax seed meal – ½ cup rice drink – pinch sea salt
4 T. Roma (coffee substitute) – 2½ cups rolled oats
2½ cups whole grain flour (spelt, oat, brown rice)
1½ cups grain sweetened chocolate chips
¾ cup chopped walnuts

Put in a food processor the olive oil, brown rice syrup, flax seed meal, rice drink, sea salt and Roma, puree until smooth. Mix together the rolled oats, flour, chocolate chips and walnuts. Add the pureed mixture and mix all together. Spoon onto an oiled cookie sheet, press down with a fork, bake at 350 degrees for 20 minutes. Makes 12 large cookies.

Pear Black Raspberry Crisp

3 pears (cut in thin slices) – 1 cup black raspberries
½ cup brown rice syrup – 3 T. arrowroot – pinch sea salt
2 T. lemon juice – 1 ½ cups cookie crumbs

Place all ingredients, except the cookie crumbs, in a sauce pan. On low heat, slowly heat the fruit filling, stirring a couple times, until it starts to thicken. Pour into an oiled casserole dish, sprinkle the cookie crumbs over the top. Bake at 350 degrees for 30 minutes.

Nutrition: Black raspberries are smaller and sweeter than blackberries. Both can be used in this recipe. Both contain fiber, antioxidants, and help cleanse the blood.

Peanut Butter Apple Treats

2 apples – 4 T. peanut butter – 1 T. rice drink
¼ tsp. cinnamon – pinch sea salt – raisins for garnish

Cut the apples in half down the middle in order for them to lay flat on a cookie sheet. Scoop out the seeds and discard them. Scoop out some of the apple to use in the stuffing. Put in a food processor the peanut butter, rice drink, cinnamon, sea salt and apple flesh. Puree until smooth. Spoon the mixture into the apple halves. Bake at 350 degrees for 30 minutes. Sprinkle some raisins over the top for garnish, serve warm.

111

Carrot Raisin Dessert Salad

8 carrots (diced medium) – 1 cup raisins – 4 T. water
1 cup pecans (roasted and chopped) – 3 tsp. olive oil
4 T. brown rice syrup – ½ tsp. cinnamon
¼ tsp. cloves – pinch sea salt

Boil the carrots for about 7 minutes until fork tender. Drain carrots, save 4 T. of cooking water to use in the recipe. Put carrots in food processor, pulse and chop the carrots up, do not over chop, the carrots will get mushy. Mix together the olive oil, brown rice syrup, cinnamon, cloves, sea salt, and 4 T. water. Mix all together the carrots, raisins, pecans, and wet mixture. Refrigerate and serve cold.

Peanut Butter and Jelly Treats

1 cup peanut butter – ½ cup brown rice syrup
2 cups crispy brown rice cereal
1 cup grain sweetened chocolate chips
1 cup your favorite fruit jam

Mix together the peanut butter, brown rice syrup and cereal. Press into an oiled casserole dish, should be ½ inch thick. On a low heat, melt the chocolate chips, stirring as it melts to prevent scorching. Spread over the peanut butter crisp. Refrigerate until cold. Spread the jam over the top. Cut and serve.

Stuffed Peaches

2 large peaches – ½ cups cashews – ¼ cup raisins
2 T. olive oil – 2 T. water – 3 T. brown rice syrup
1 T. barley malt* – additional ¼ cup chopped cashews
      Cut peaches in half and remove pits. Scoop out some of the flesh and save for stuffing. Put in a food processor the peach flesh, ½ cup cashews and raisins, puree until smooth. Stuff the peach halves with the pureed mixture. Place then in a casserole dish that has a lid. Heat on low, in a sauce pan the, olive oil, water, brown rice syrup and barley malt for about 7 minutes. Pour sauce over the stuffed peaches, bake covered, 350 degrees for20 minutes. Serve with the additional ¼ cup chopped cashews sprinkled over the top.
      <u>Nutrition:</u> Sweet and juicy, peaches are high in vitamin A and C and calcium.
      *Substitute brown rice syrup for barley malt to make gluten free.

Pear Pudding

4 cups rice drink – 6 T. agar flakes – pinch sea salt
2 pears (peeled and cut up) – ½ cup brown rice syrup
3 T. kudzu (dissolved in ¼ cup water)

Put in a pot the rice drink, agar flakes, sea salt, pears and brown rice syrup. Bring to a boil, reduce heat and simmer for 15 minutes. Whisk in the dissolved kudzu and continue to simmer for 5 minutes. It will thicken as it heats. Pour into a dish and refrigerate until cold. Put in food processor and puree until smooth. Pour into cups and serve.

Vanilla Pudding

6 cups rice drink – 1 cup brown rice syrup – pinch sea salt
4 T. agar flakes – 3 T. kudzu (dissolved in ¼ cup water)
1 T. vanilla

Put in a pot the rice drink, agar flakes, sea salt, and brown rice syrup. Bring to a boil, reduce heat and simmer for 15 minutes. Whisk in the dissolved kudzu and continue to simmer for 5 minutes. It will thicken as it heats. Pour into a dish and refrigerate until cold. Put in food processor and puree until smooth. Pour into cups and serve.

~Thank You, God~

Thank you God for everything today
The sun shining, all the birds singing
The trees swaying in the wind
The warm shower this cold morning
All the delicious food I whole heartedly consume
The shiny new penny, I found on the ground
All the people who cross my path
And the wondrous time I spent with myself
For this miraculous place Earth, I call home
I stand in deep appreciation
Today and every day.

Glossary

Aduki beans – small red bean, helps to strengthen your kidneys

Agar flakes – sea vegetable in flake form, used to gel liquids

Al Dente – cooked for a short period of time so food is still crisp

Almond Butter – almonds crushed into a smooth paste

Amazake – thick, sweet, fermented beverage made from sweet brown rice and koji, will not spike blood sugar

Arame – black, shredded sea vegetable, high in calcium and protein

Arrowroot – white powder that is used to thicken sauces and desserts

Barley – the signature whole grain of spring, helps break down fat in your system

Barley malt – whole grain sweetener made from barley, will not spike blood sugar

Brown rice – signature whole grain of fall, nutritional superior to white rice

Brown rice syrup – whole grain sweetener made from whole brown rice, best sugar substitute, does not spike blood sugar

Brown rice vinegar – gently tart, sweet vinegar made from fermented whole brown rice

Burdock – brown, root vegetable, good for your skin and as a blood purifier

Chick peas – also knows as garbanzo beans, creamy, sweet bean high in vitamin C

Chocolate chips, grain sweetened – chips that are sugar and dairy free, sweetened with whole grain sweeteners, barley and corn (chocolate is not recommended on a healing, or limited macrobiotic diet)

Daikon – long, white, root vegetable, in the radish family, not as pungent tasting as red radish

Dulse – purple, reddish sea vegetable, high in iron and helps strengthen the adrenal glands

Flaxseed meal – ground up flax seeds, used as an egg substitute in desserts help the rising action

Green Lentils – small, green bean from the legume family, high in protein, calcium, and fiber

Kale – leafy, green vegetable, high in vitamin C, calcium, iron and protein

Kasha – signature whole grain of winter, the kasha kernel is ground up and becomes buckwheat flour

Kombu – dark green sea vegetable, always used in cooking beans to make them more digestible and help eliminate gas

Kudzu – thick root that is sold in white chunks, used to thicken sauces, very medicinal and helps alkalize your system

Maple syrup – natural sweetener used as a sugar replacement

Millet – signature whole grain of late summer, small, yellow kernels, creamy texture

Mirin – sweet brown rice cooking wine

Miso – naturally fermented soybean paste, salty seasoning, very medicinal

> **Dark miso** – fermented for at least two years, darker in color and a stronger salty taste
>
> **Mellow miso** – fermented for only one year, lighter in color and sweeter to the taste

Mochi – whole food make from pounded sweet brown rice, sold in refrigerator in a block, when cooked it has a sticky texture

Pine Nuts – small white nuts comes from pine trees

Pot boil – to boil in a pot on stove with lid on

Quinoa – signature whole grain of summer, high in protein, supports heart and brain

Radicchio –small red head of lettuce

Rice drink – non-dairy beverage make from brown rice

Roma – coffee substitute made from malted barley, roasted barley, chicory and rye, no caffeine

Sea salt – salt that has not been refined and retains all its minerals and trace minerals

Sea vegetables – sea weeds grown in ocean

Shiitake mushrooms – Japanese mushroom, helps to cleanse toxins out of your system

Silken tofu – tofu that has a smooth texture, used to make desserts

Tahini – paste made from ground sesame seeds

Tamari – wheat free, salty condiment, made from naturally fermented soybeans (healthy version of soy sauce)

Tempeh – textured, soy food, made from fermented soybeans, high in protein

Toasted sesame oil – unrefined, pure pressed, sesame oil that has a smoky or toasted flavor

Tofu – white, soy food, high in calcium and protein

Ume plum paste – Umeboshi plum paste – thick, red paste made from naturally fermented plums, Japanese salty condiment, very medicinal

Ume vinegar – salty brine from making ume plum paste

Vegenaise – dairy free, sugar free, vegan mayonnaise

Wild Rice – wild seed, considered a whole grain

Yellow split peas – yellow version of split peas

Index of Recipes

~ *A Big Turn* ~

If life knocks you off your feet
Get up and scratch your seat
If you can't seem to rebound
Then it must be really profound
If it all seems to be lost
Don't give up at any cost
Life is about ready to make a big turn
To show you what you must learn
So keep on the right track
And remember how you made your pact
About the life you swore you would never give up
Not even when the worst of things keep showing up
So lift yourself up off the ground
And turn your life completely around.

Made in the USA
Middletown, DE
05 December 2017